SURF 1

THE
LIGHT-LINE
REVOLUTION

2nd Edition

SURF FISHING

THE LIGHT-LINE REVOLUTION

2nd *Edition*

A Shore Fisherman's Guide To Fishing The Surf

Bill Varney, Jr.

www.fishthesurf.com
Long Beach, CA

The information contained in this book was compiled over a lifetime and is meant to be used as a guide to ocean surf fishing.

This book contains information gathered from several sources and has been reviewed and edited. The publisher, author and editors do not guarantee the book's accuracy and assume no responsibility for injury or property damage resulting from the use of this book's contents.

Because fishing, as with most sports, is inherently dangerous become familiar with your equipment, watch the weather and be respectful and cognizant of your surroundings.

Copyright ©2010 by Bill Varney Jr.
All rights reserved
No part of this book may be used or reproduced in any manner whatsoever without the written permission of the publisher, except for the inclusion of a brief quotation in a review.

Written, printed and published in the United States of America
"God Bless Her"

Written by: Bill Varney, Jr
Executive Editor: Brad Baier

Books available at:
www.fishthesurf.com
Bill Varney, Jr.
4501 E. Pacific Coast Hwy.
Long Beach, CA 90804
(714) 377-9001

ISBN: 978-0-9772486-1-2

Second Edition

To my wife Kristen,
For her immeasurable patience
To my father
For his introduction to the ocean
To my mother for her support of my dreams
And to my kids and all children
For their contagious enthusiasm to learn everything the sea has to offer.

Written by Bill Varney, Jr.

Executive Editor Brad Baier

Contributing Editors:
Brad Baier
Arthur Lai
Dana Rea
Andre Weckstrom

Field Research Group:
Brad, Ken, Kevin, Bill, Behdad, Ed, et. Al.

Table of Contents

Preface

Quotes

Introduction.. 1

   1. Light-Line Surf Gear... 3
      Gear for sandy beaches
      Fishing sandy beaches
      Gear for rocky shores
      Fishing rocky shores

   2. Surf Rigging... 24
      Lines and leaders
      Sinkers
      Swivels
      Hooks
      Beads
      Knot tying
      Rigging

   3. Bait.. 47
      Types of bait
      Catching bait
      Keeping bait alive
      Hooking various baits
      Freezing and storing bait

   4. Types of Surf Fish...86
      Types of surf fish
      Strikes
      Best baits
      Best spots
      Rig up

5. Surf Fishing Techniques for California Halibut........................ 107

6. Taking Control... 124
   Fighting the fish
   Fishing in the wind

7. Tide And Moon.. 129
   What causes tides
   What tide is best for surf fishing
   How to read tide charts
   Tides and the time of day
   The moon's affect on surf fishing

8. Catch And Release... 136
   How to safely release fish
   Surf fishing etiquette

9. Surf Fishing Road Trips... 141
   Jalama Beach Park
   Refugio State Beach
   Emma Woods State Beach
   Bolsa Chica State Beach
   South Carlsbad State Beach

Appendix
   I   Preparing For The Beach... 153
   II How-to build a Ghost Shrimp Pump............................. 159
   III Tackle Shops With Surf Bait....................................... 172
   IV California State Records.. 174

Surf Fish Calendar.. 176

Surf Bait Calendar.. 177

References... 178

<u>Surf Fishing, The Light-Line Revolution's</u> first copyrighted edition in 2006 was a great success but left a lot of uncharted surf fishing know-how; So I called upon our top-notch field research team to take another look at the beach and compile more tips, tricks and up-to-date information to help us become better surf fisherman.

This edition is packed with updates on existing techniques, newly discovered baits, bolder, bigger illustrations and some of the places I love to fish along our coast.

Back in the late 1980's we were beginning to explore the light-line technique. Since then we have learned a great deal more and have been assisted by new and ever improving equipment from all across the globe.

Because surf fishing resembles lake fishing, the crossover of rigging, baits and technique has been astounding. In my book I explore ideas on what techniques have worked for me and hope this will help others to enjoy the beach too. Additionally, don't be afraid to try something new. This is how most of fishing's greatest secrets were discovered.

Please contact me with your surf fishing questions, comments, reports and pictures. I can be reached by email at: <u>fishthesurf@mail.com</u>. Also, be sure to stay up-to-date by visiting my site: <u>www.fishthesurf.com</u> where you'll find tons of tips and tricks to make you a better surf fisherman.

Light winds, tight lines and good fishing,
Bill

FISHING QUOTES

There's a fine line between fishing and just standing on the shore like an idiot. ~Steven Wright

It has always been my private conviction that any man who pits his intelligence against a fish and loses has it coming. ~John Steinbeck

"Fishing is a discipline in the equality of men, for all men are equal before fish."
Herbert Hoover

"If I fished only to capture fish, my fishing trips would have ended long ago." Zane Grey

"The charm of fishing is that it is the pursuit of something that is elusive but attainable, a perpetual series of occasions for hope."
John Buchan

"Never leave fish to find fish" Moses, 1200BC

"Of all the world's enjoyments that ever valued were, there's none of our employments with fishing can compare!"
Thomas D'urfey

*We ask a simple question
And that is all we wish:
Are fishermen all liars?
Or do only liars fish?
~William Sherwood Fox, <u>Silken Lines and Silver Hooks</u>, 1954*

Many men go fishing all of their lives without knowing that it is not fish they are after. ~Henry David Thoreau

*"I'd rather be fishing"
Jimmy L. Glass
Louisiana electric chair, 1987*

INTRODUCTION

In the beginning:
Oh boy, it's sure a long way down! The sun is beginning to set and it's every color in the world. As dad reels the line up it comes over the edge with one, two, three bare hooks and suddenly a jumpy little fish. I'm three, and my dad is patiently trying to teach me how to fish from the Redondo Monstad Pier.

Most other days, we'd stop by Jerry's Tackle Box or Red's, get bait, our long rods and go fishing at the beach. Dad would put a three ounce pyramid sinker on the line and cast it out as far as the eye could see. Occasionally, we caught a good fish, but most of the time it was kelp and fought like a sinking car.

Later on:
In the dark, shortly before the sun began to rise, I would ride my bike to the pier to fish for surfperch. The butt of my rod was fastened inside and "Alpo" dog food can bolted to the right side of

my front tire. On my back was a knapsack crammed full of tackle and food.

Once there, we'd climb under the pier and fish up against the pilings for perch. One day, when we ran out of bait. I pulled a sidewinder crab from the piling, pinned it on the hook, and let my line out. Upon hitting the water, a shadow swam out from under the dock, clamped onto the crab, and almost pulled me into the water.

Today:

I'm scrambling up the rocks because a big wave is coming and I know I'll get wet. I'm older and a lot slower but it's OK, my gear is light and I'm out of the wave's path in time.

It's a work day and almost everyone's at the job but me. I have the whole beach to myself. Today I'm fishing with the lightest gear possible. My rod is eight feet long and weighs only twenty-ounces. I use four pound pink line on a reel that almost fits in my front pocket. All the gear and bait I'll ever need is in a small hook wallet hanging around my neck.

Sorry, it's time to go now. **Yeah ! I think I'm getting a bite**...

Take everything you learn from this book and expand upon it. Do feel free to try your own fishing experiments and refine your light-line technique. The knowledge you'll learn from this book was compiled from years of local surf fishing and a lot of good people who were brave enough to share what they know with all of us.

As a teenager my education continued thanks to the help of notable fisherman Jerry Morris, Fred Oakley, Hap Jacobs, John Dipley, Pineapple, Wesley Strong, Red and the owners of *TC Bait and Tackle* where I worked.

Tight lines and good fishing,
Bill

CHAPTER 1

Surf Gear

In This Chapter

Gear for Sandy Beaches
Fishing Sandy Beaches
Gear for Rocky Shores
Fishing Rocky Shores

Let's first get started by looking at two of my favorite rod and reel combinations: One for sandy beaches with limited rocks and another for rocky areas such as jetties and breakwalls.

GEAR FOR SANDY BEACHES

On sandy beaches there is less chance of entanglement with structure so you can fish much lighter gear and line. I suggest using a 6 to 8 foot spinning rod (i.e. trout/steelhead rod) with a line rating of 4-14lb pound test. This is the best surf rod for casting, feeling the strike and fighting the fish. Limber rods help the angler with retrieval by keeping the line taught as the fish is brought in through the incoming surf. Look for a rod with a stiff reel seat, rigid butt section and a limber tip.

Your spinning reel should have a minimum line capacity of 200 yards of four-pound monofilament (good examples would be Shimano® 2000 and 2500 series reels). Keeping your rod and reel light is important because you will be walking the beach searching for fish and you'll want to stay light on your feet. Because you're on the move, use a hook keeper near the reel seat to hold the hook safe and securely.

This will also help to prevent your line from becoming tangled and/or wrapping around your rod tip as you walk between different areas. Less time wasted untangling equals more time with your bait in the water.

I spool up with 4 or 6 pound test mono. My favorite colors are pink and red. Pink and red are not everyone's first choice, but their color closely resembles sediment-jumbled water. Because of its stretch and strength pink 4 to 6lb pound test Ande® or red 4 to 6 pound Stren® are my lines of choice. I use these colors for two reasons.

First, in the color spectrum, red light has the longest wavelength in the visible light spectrum and as such is the first color to diffuse underwater due to refraction. It is this property that may make red the color that fish seem to find the most difficult to see—especially in the foaming water of the surf. Secondly, when surf fishing it is imperative to be able to see where you line is at all times. You may be fishing close to rocks or in a specific trough or hole. Being able to see your line you will be able to direct your bait to an area of fewer snags and more fish.

FISHING THE BEACH

Never are the rules of observation more important than in fishing. The best and most productive fishermen pay special attention to water, tide and weather conditions. I like to call it the 3 W's: **Wind**, **Waves** and **Water**.

Here are three questions to ask when looking for the best place to fish at the beach:
What direction is the *wind* blowing?
What is the size and direction of the *waves*?
Where is the *water* clear, cloudy, cool or warm?

Which direction is the *wind* blowing?
Knowing wind direction and intensity are important when fishing the beach. Ideal conditions would be a slight offshore breeze or no wind at all. You'll find these conditions usually in the morning or near sunset. Don't forget about mild Santa Ana wind days. They may provide perfect conditions all day. On days like this you can use the lightest tackle and still keep your bait on the bottom. On windy days you'll have to go to a heavier sinker and sometimes walk with your line down the beach to keep your bait on the bottom.

What is the size and direction of the *waves*?
Wave size and direction is always a big factor in where and when to fish. If the surf is too big it's impossible to catch fish because the current and surge are moving too fast. Look for days with waves no bigger than 4 feet. If the surf is large try to find protected areas near rocks or inside a shoreline point to fish.

Don't be surprised that you might also find poor fishing on a day when the surf is flat. Fish always seek moving water to churn up bait, create troughs and also eddies that they can use as ambush points.

The direction of the swell will tell you where to start when fishing near points, bays, reefs and rock structures like jetties or harbor entrances. Winter storms will always bring West and Northwest surf (creating waves breaking from the North toward the South). Summer storms usually come with surf from the South and Southwest (creating powerful waves breaking from the South to the North)

Winter storms will remove sand from the face of the beach and deposit it off shore creating bars and troughs. Summer waves generally re-deposit the sand back up the face of the beach. Swell direction also has a direct correlation with the long-shore current. This is the direction in which your bait will travel along the beach. Take note as to how the swell direction effects the areas you like to fish. This will let you know when they are at their best.

Where is the *water* clear, cloudy, cool or warm?
Is the water clear or cloudy? This is the first thing I check once I get to the beach. Clear water is great but most fish don't like it. Certain fish like the corbina love clear water because they rely on sight to capture sand crabs when they become exposed for the short duration of time between being dislodged from the sand by wave action and burrowing themselves back into the sand. But

most fish avoid clear water when they have a choice. They will seek a place with more privacy and a chance to hide. Any fish in clear shallow water is vulnerable to predators.

In most cases foamy, cloudy water is what surf fish like. I look for the areas where clear meets dirty water and try to fish the edge where they converge. Look for these conditions near rip tides, troughs, river mouths and jetties.

Cool and warm water conditions let you know what bait to use and how to use it. In cold winter conditions grubs work well for surf fish. Colder water retards a fish's metabolism as they perfer a much slower bait presentation. They also don't seem to be as "line shy" this time of year. This may be due to a reduction in forage in colder months.

In the summer when the water is warm, surf fish key in on natural baits. Fish feed voraciously in the spring, summer and fall just before spawning. At these times, they are looking for natural baits and realistic lures that mimic the baits of an area. Pay special attention to what occurs around you in both the sand and on the rocks. If you find sand crabs in the sand or mussel on the rocks, you can be well assured that is what the fish are eating.

What to do once you've made it to the beach...
Once on the beach, surf fishermen must observe beach conditions and determine where the best spot to fish is. Unlike boat fishing, where it may be as easy as finding a rock to anchor over and catch fish, more subtle observations are required at the beach. Once you learn to recognize them you can be assured you will know where the fish are.

When you get to the beach you want to find an area where you can get a good view of the water line. Standing on the beach's berm above the waves is a good place to start. Take a few minutes to look up and down the beach. First, look at the beach itself and see how it curves into the water at the shoreline. If you look carefully you will see areas that are points and areas, which are bays. The surf, current and tidal movement, will create both small and large points and bays.

Subtle differences like these help point out where the fish are living and feeding. Inshore troughs and rip currents working in conjunction with beach points and bays to make for some of the best fishing spots.

Remember that fish move and gather in schools to feed. I always start by fan casting. That is casting to my left, straight out, and to my right at multiple angles to cover as much ocean as possible. If I don't get a bite it's time to move and work my way up or down the beach. Try moving 100 yards at a time and continue fan-casting motion to locate feeding fish. Always keep your eyes on the waves and the water as you move between different areas. Some subtle difference in water color, or how the waves are breaking, may be the clue you are looking for that leads you to active fish.

The Inshore Trough

If you're looking straight out to sea--the inshore trough is 20 to 60 feet in front of you running parallel to the beach. It's usually about six to ten feet wide and two feet deep. In larger surf areas the trough will be more pronounced.

The trough is created by the pounding shore break and is the perfect place for fish to hide and search for food. Corbina prowl in wait in the trough and will rush up the beach with wreakless abandon to eat sand crabs. Surfperch drift suspended in the trough and feed on churned up crabs, worms, shrimp and clams.

Generally, two troughs will form. One created by the inside shore break, mostly during high tide and another formed by sets of waves breaking farther offshore when the tide is low. The most effective time to fish the inner trough is during high tide periods when it is well under water. The best time to fish the outer trough is at low tide, when the fish move offshore and into the outer trough to feed and hide. The distance between the inshore and outer trough is dependant on the angle that the sandy bottom slopes away toward deeper water. The more gradual the slope the farther out the outside trough will be.

I like to fish the inner trough for surfperch and corbina. While at low tide, it's great to wade through the inner trough and out to the sandbar so I can fish the outer trough and beyond. Fishing the outer waters has always been productive for halibut and yellowfin croaker. Casting lures like Luhr Jensen's Krocodile® or the Lucky Craft Flash Minnow® have always worked well to bring fish up from the deeper water and onto your hook.

One of the best times to find the inshore trough on your favorite beach is at low tide. Choose a day when you can go to the beach at low tide, the lower the tide the better. Walk the beach and find the troughs. Some may be subtle, only a few feet wide or long. Others may be huge and stretch hundreds of feet. Mark the areas by looking back toward shore and lining it up with a permanent objects or landmarks. Your next step is to return at high tide and fish. Once you've lined up your spots you'll usually find it's productive and be glad you took some time for field research. Thereafter, check the spots occasionally at low tide as the beach can quickly reform and fill in yesterday's trough.

Rip Tide Conditions

Rip currents form when a set of consecutive waves pushes a large volume of water up onto the face of the beach. The "stacked up" water will rush away form the beach and create an offshore current. It appears with off-colored swirling water, with rippled areas and possibly foam. Some rips may be vigorous and obvious while others are subtle. Rip currents may form over a period of hours or appear in just minutes. Take time to scour the water while you're fishing and look for the beginning of new rip currents. Approach these areas and cast along their sides. Retrieve you bait slowly in these areas as fish will be swimming in and out of the churning water looking for food.

Rip currents normally extend twice or three times as far out as the surf break itself. As they channel water out and away from land, they may also create a trough perpendicular to the shore. Fish wait near this offshore trough for bait churned up by the rough waters. If you locate a rip channel that cuts across the inshore trough, take additional time to fish the zone where they intersect.

A rip current will pull objects away from the beach and out to sea. On each side of the rip is a neutral pocket formed by an eddy circulation. This eddy makes the rip current the shape of a mushroom.

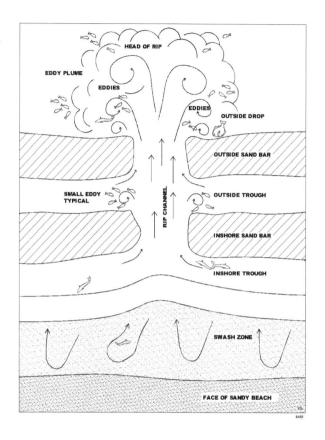

Fish the outside edges of a rip current

Tip:
The best place to fish a rip current is on its sides. Cast out and retrieve your bait back along the current's edges and toward shore. Fish will also hide and feed in the area near the top of the mushroom, on the very outer edge, or "head" of the rip.

Rip current conditions can also be created by beach dredging equipment. The water that can stack up on the beach will follow the path of least resistance, which may be a channel created by mechanical dredging. As the dredge re-deposits sand, it churns up bait and attracts fish. Try fishing along the edges of an area being dredged where turbid water meets clear water. Use the same technique as with a rip current of casting and retrieving your bait along its edges.

Points And Bays
The beach is made up of various points and bays. Some may be hundreds of yards wide or as small as just a few yards apart. Water circulates around these areas and creates fishing opportunities.

Take the vantage point above the shore break and look down the beach in each direction. Where on the beach
does the sand extend up and out toward the surf? This is the point.

Point in foreground bay in background

Look and see were the beach comes in and the water floods up the beach in a low area. This is the bay.

The best place to fish on a point is along its sides where the water slows down as the bottom drops off. Waves break along a point in a triangle. The best place to fish is along the edge of the triangle shape. This is where fish forage as the current created by the breaking waves slows down and releases the bait and particles it carries. Points are usually productive areas for walleye surfperch and barred surfperch.

Foam triangle

When fishing the bay, remember that the water and current are moving much slower. Your bait will have much less natural action so slow retrieval is a must. Be sure to keep in contact with the bottom at all times with your line tight.

An inshore trough running parallel to the beach in a bay is productive for corbina and perch. Try retrieving your bait not only across the trough but also along it by walking down the beach and fan casting at various angles. This will keep your bait in the strike-zone longer.

Winter And Summer Sand Conditions

Southern California beaches make a remarkable transformation each year as the seasons change and the long-shore current and swells reshape our coastline.

In the summer, swells from the south and southwest push sand northward and onto the beaches. Most areas will gain about forty feet of new sand each summer. This number will be exaggerated in years where strong south swells, generated by hurricanes in Mexico and winter storms in the South Pacific, push even more sand onto our beaches.

This softer sand becomes the home of the sand crab and worm. It reshapes the coastline and accentuates the points and bays described above. Softer sand also allows for a deeper and wider inshore trough.

The summer sands, and warmer water temperatures, bring their own style of fishing. Crabs are more abundant and the fish that eat them, such as the corbina, will venture into the shallowest water to find them. Look for some of your best fishing in the inshore trough during the summer season.

Winter beach erosion

During the winter, storms produce powerful waves from the West that erode the beach. The sand recedes from the beach uncovering hidden structure. This provides excellent feeding opportunities and becomes home to surfperch and yellowfin croaker. From December through May, go to your favorite beaches at low tide and find the areas where sand has eroded away to expose rock and plant habitat. Throughout winter, fish these spots during a rising high tide and you'll find them to be your most productive fishing areas.

FISHING GEAR FOR ROCKY SHORES

When surf fishing in areas with jetties and break wall rocks, you'll encounter new challenges that require a change in equipment. Because the chance of entanglement with structure is inevitable your gear must match your surroundings.

Upsize your equipment with an 8-9' rod rated for 6-18 pound test; a steelhead rod works well. I use an eight and one-half foot spinning rod. Once again the tip must be limber to feel the strike, set the hook and get untangled from rocks. Your reel should have a minimum line capacity of two hundred forty yards of 8 to 12 pound monofilament line (a 2500-4000 series is a good reel size).

I spool up with 8 to 12 pound test line; my favorite colors are red, pink or green. I use 10 or 12 pound fluorocarbon leaders because they are both abrasion resistant (which is important when you're near the rocks) and invisible to fish. Fluorocarbon line has the same specific gravity, or density, as water and as such light does not refract when passing through it, making it invisible.

A longer and stiffer rod will allow you to cast more weight and be able to pull fish away from and over the rocks. You have a much better chance of hooking a much larger fish from the rocks. Go one time unprepared and you may lose the fish of a lifetime!

Fishing From The Rocks
Rocks and rock jetties come in all shapes and sizes. A series of rocks creates an eddy circulation found in rip currents. The outcropping of rock creates an eddy circulation around its point. This is where currents create a natural feeding habitat due to the water movement caused by waves and tidal changes. Eddies that form at rock structures are more predictable, and therefore easier to locate, than eddies formed by rip currents.

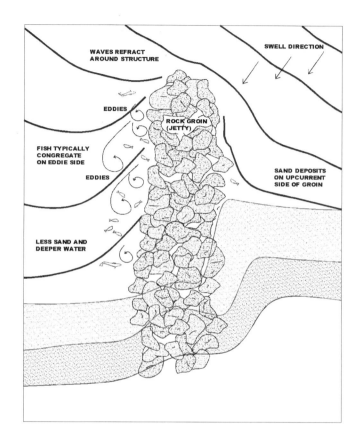

As the tide moves up and down throughout the day water currents vary in strength and intensity. At slack tides, only the wave action will be working to produce eddy currents. Very little water will be moving around rock points associated with harbor entrances, river mouths and estuaries. During larger tidal movements more water will be moving creating considerable eddy circulation.

Surf and swell direction also have an effect on eddies that occur near jetties and groins (a groin is man-made rock jetty or plates of steel oriented perpendicular to the beach, designed to reduce

). Swell direction will also drive the long shore current. slack tides, the long shore current may create an eddy on the down-current side of the rocks. By rule, the larger the swell the stronger and more pronounced water movement will be.

Eddy circulation is critical to fishing because it provides a current where fish can suspend themselves with a minimum of effort, while water flushes through their gills providing additional oxygen. The eddy also provides a current that will capture and collect bait and nutrients and bring them within the fishes' strike zone.

Slack tide conditions create very little circulation and require fish to move from area to area to seek oxygen rich waters and search for food. Fishing is always best when there is a slow to moderate current condition. Conditions of no current or a very strong one are least productive and make fishing tough.

Once upon the rocks, or rock area you'll be fishing, look out toward the point and find the leeward or down current side of the structure. This will many times be the side of the rocks opposite the direction of swells. Watch closely for the direction of the current. Look for similar characteristics to the rip current: swirling dirty water, rippled areas and possible foam.

Fish the outside and inside edges of the eddy. The outside edge may be toward open water and the inside up against the rocks. This is where the fish will hide, breathing comfortably and waiting for their next meal.

Fish don't like to swim in the fastest moving portion of an eddy. They prefer to stay on the sidelines and wait for your bait!

Unlike most *beach* surf fishing, fishing from the rocks is productive at both high and low tides.

Tip:

Look for these things when you reach the beach: Riptides, triangle waves patterns, inshore and offshore troughs and holes created by churning waves. Fish these areas as they are home to foraging surf fish.

When fishing the rocks find the leeward side of the jetty and fish the eddy. It will appear much like a riptide with foaming, dirty, churning water.

Fan cast as you move down the beach so that your bait can cover more area. Once you find the fish try several baits to see what works best.

Look for bait that occurs naturally at the beach you are fishing and try to replicate those baits using the same colors and sizes. This works surprisingly well with both natural and artificial baits.

CHAPTER 2

Surf Rigging

In This Chapter

Lines And Leaders
Sinkers
Swivels
Hooks
Beads
Knot tying
Rigging

This chapter is dedicated to the craft of the surf rig. A lot has changed from the days when we employed the dropper loop and a four-ounce pyramid sinker "cluster bomb"! Today's surf fishermen use lighter and more selective tackle to target the most exciting species of surf fish.

Terminal Tackle

Terminal tackle includes line, sinker, bead , swivel, leader and hook or lure.

Lines And Leaders

To prepare your rigging you'll need some terminal tackle. The first items to consider are line and leader material. The monofilament on your spinning reel should be strong and flexible. I prefer Ande or Stren line in pink or red.

There are several reasons why I like to use this high visibility monofilament. First, monofilament offers stretch and cushion against the push and pull of the surf. Braided lines may offer incredible sensitivity but they don't stretch and make it hard to land a fish in a strong current without pulling the hook.

Visibility is also an important factor. Improving your ability to see where your line is in relation to rocks, inshore troughs, holes and breezing fish, will increase your likeliness of success. Red is a great color for us to see but a tough color for fish to discern in the surf.

Lines like Ande® , Maxima®, Stren® and Berkley® all work well because they stretch and act like a shock absorber. This is critical when you are attempting to haul a large fish across the inshore trough and into shore. Stiffer lines tend to kink easily and can snap under load when pounded by waves. Line test recommendations are four to six pound test for sandy beaches and eight to twelve pound test for rocky shores.

When spooling your spinning reel with monofilament, always feed the new line off the end of the spool and onto your reel. By placing the new spool on its side, (usually label side up) the new line will have a slight twist and explode off the reel while casting. *(see diagram below)*

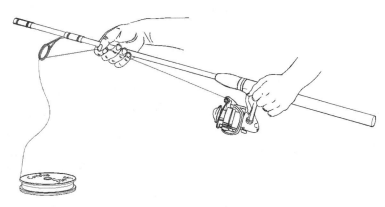

Start with the line spool laying flat with the label side up. The line is wound onto the reel in the direction that it uncoils to reduce line twist. Tie a uni-knot loop in the end of the line and trim the knot before you attach it to the reel spool. Be certain that you thread the line through the first guide on the rod and that the reel bail is open. Pull the loop taught onto the spool and close the bail. Tighten the drag to 100 % of the pound test and hold the line up near the guide to produce tension as the line winds onto the spool.

Watch your line carefully as you fill the reel; the line should loop loosely off the spool. If the line coils get smaller as you wind, your line will twist too much. When this occurs turn the spool over (usually label side down) and continue until the loops are relaxed. Your reel is full when the line is within 1/16th of an inch from the edge of the spool. A full reel will cast farther because there is less resistance as the line flows off. After filling the reel, back the drag off completely, if you are not fishing immediately, to prevent damage to your washers.

TIP
Wet your line with a spray bottle or splash of fresh water before fishing. This will help the line flow off the reel and reduce tangles.

As you prepare to fish set your drag to one-half of the pound test rating on your line or leader, whichever has the lowest rating. A convenient way to set your drag is with a spring scale typically used to weigh fish. Also, practice setting your drag by hand; once set, pull some line off paying attention to the resistance of line coming off the spool. In no time it will be easy to find the perfect setting for your reel.

Several factors will determine how long your line will last. Reels kept out of the sun and washed off with fresh water will always last longer. Never leave your reels in the car or the trunk in the heat. After each trip to the beach rinse your outfit off with a soft spray from the hose or a misting bottle and dry off immediately. This helps eliminate the salt and sand build up on your line, reel and rod. Before rinsing your equipment you should tighten the drag snug to keep water, sand and salt out of your drag system.

I use a quart spray bottle filled with two tablespoons of dish soap and water to wash off my rod and reel, followed by a fresh water rinse. An old white cotton sock over your hand works well to dry off your rig. I also spray a small amount of lubricant (c.f. Corrosion X®) on a sock and wipe down the reel to leave it with a thin oil coating to protect and lubricate.

You'll know that it's time to replace your line when you experience the following:

Line loses color and becomes a milky shade

Line has memory and begins to curl and stay curled

Line has less stretch and becomes brittle and breaks easily

Line surface is rough and uneven when you run it through your fingers

Leader Material

Under most circumstances a fluorocarbon leader is matched to the pound test rating of your main line. Exceptions may include "line shy" fish where a lighter leader is used to entice the fish to bite, or when targeting larger fish a heavier leader may be employed if you get bitten off. Clear fluorocarbon is preferred as pigments added may weaken the line.

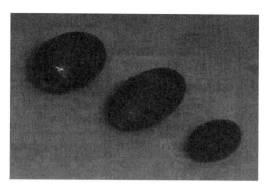

Sinkers

Egg sinkers and split shot sinkers are the most commonly used surf weights. Egg sinkers weighing one-eighth to one ounce are the most useful sizes for light-line fishing. Remember to use heavier sinkers in strong drift, wind and large surf conditions. Smaller sinkers are best for calm days and give your bait the most life-like movement. Use the lightest weight that you can fish effectively. This will improve the sensitivity transmitted to your rod when the fish picks up your bait.

Another application for the egg sinker is when fishing near rocks. Use the lightest sinker possible (1/8th oz) and you'll get snagged less and have a better chance to un-snag your weight when it's jammed between rocks. Small diameter Mojo® sinkers are another useful alternative near rocks.

Egg sinkers work particularly well in the surf because their freedom of movement on the line. This helps when pulling the fish through the surf. It allows you to feel the fish pick up your bait without the fish feeling the resistance of the sinker as the line freely slides through it. Additionally, egg sinkers will dig into the sand, especially during the retrieve, kicking up a plume that attracts the fish to whatever is trailing behind.

A split shot or pinch on Gremlin® weight can be used with sand crabs for targeting corbina. This method uses the ocean's surge to roll the bait in and out, with the swash of the waves, in shallow water where corbina feed. This technique is much like "flylining" a live bait.

Beads

Beads come in several sizes. A 6mm bead to 8mm is used between the sliding sinker and the swivel, protecting your knot. It allows the sinker to move more freely so as not to bind or chafe the line.

As a fish attractant, 4mm beads can be used on the leader, just above the hook when fishing with sand crabs or grubs. The most productive colors are red and orange bead, although a variety of colors, as well as clear, may work under differing conditions.

I can't explain the physics exactly but without the bead sand will be deposited into the egg sinker and keep it from sliding. Bound by sand, light line is sure to break. I like to use a red or orange bead in winter to attract breeding surfperch. In summer, I'll use a clear bead for a stealth presentation to target cruising corbina.

Swivels

Swivels are used as the connection between your leader and the main line. They act as a stop for the bead and sinker by keeping them well above the hook. Use the smallest swivel possible.

I use number 10, 12 and 14 swivels (#14 being the smallest). Also, black rather than brass swivels seem to work best because they look like a grain of sand and don't reflect light which may scare fish away.

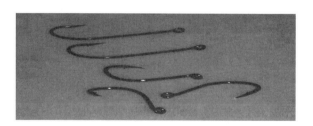

Hooks

There are two basic surf hooks I utilize: *Long shank worm hooks* and *thin wire bait hooks.*

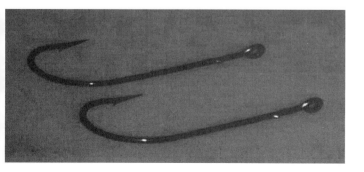

Long shank hooks, like sproat or kahle hooks, work great in the surf. The longer shaft makes it easier to pull the eye up and through the worm. Most worm hooks also have a series of barbs on the shaft that help keep bait on the hook and your "pants" from being pulled down.

I use a size #1 for larger baits and #2 for smaller baits. Long shank hooks also work well with larger plastic grubs, ghost shrimp, large sidewinder crabs and mussel. Black/non zinc hooks rust faster in your tackle bag but disintegrate by rusting out quickly when they need to be left in a fish.

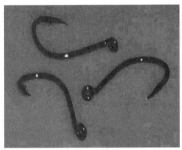

Thin wire bait hooks like Gamagatsu's® drop shot/split shot hooks, Mustad® drop shot, Owner® mosquito hooks and octopus hooks are best for sand crabs, grubs, clams and small sidewinders.

Match the hook size to the size of the bait. Small crabs will require a size #6 hook. Larger sand crabs could require a #1. I pre-tie several leader rigs for easy changing. This is best accomplished when you are at home under a good light and not at the beach in the early morning darkness of a good bite.

I use 6 pound fluorocarbon for two reasons:
First, we are told this line is invisible to fish—which I tend to believe. Fluorocarbon line has a specific gravity, or density, that is slightly different than that of water. This means that there is only minute light refraction as light passes through the line when

submerged, making it virtually invisible. Second, fluorocarbon is very abrasion resistant and allows your leader to rub against rocks and chafe without breaking. Check you leader frequently for nicks or other damage, especially after catching a large fish, and replace it if in question.

Leaders are kept on a leader holder that fits in your pocket. Leader holders can be purchased at your local tackle shop or made from cardboard or plastic. Just cut a 3"x5" piece make several ½" slices spaced 1" apart in the tip and bottom edges along the long sides. Pre-tie your leaders with a terminal loop; slide the line into the top notch and pull the loop know snug to the card. You then wrap your leader around the card using the aligned notches to you're your leaders straight and untangled. Poke the hook into the card and place into a plain envelope. You can write the pound test and the date the leaders were tied on the cards and create a wide variety that will be ready in an instant. When ready to fish slip the loop end through the swivel, unwind the leader and pass the hook through the loop. Moisten the line, pull the knot through and you're ready to fish.

Tip:
The wily corbina's keen eyesight requires that you use a hook small enough to be hidden from sight inside the bait. The most important part of your surf rig is the hook. Make sure it's as sharp as possible and you're guaranteed to catch more fish.

Hooks are best kept in their original package. Do not return a hook to the pack if it has touched salt water. The salt will react and begin the rust process on all the hooks it touches. Hooks also need to be kept sharp. You can reuse hooks and leaders, but after a couple of visits to the beach, throw them out. Once engaged in salt water and sunshine hooks will immediately begin to break down.

I have been asked many times why someone gets so many bites but hooks so few fish? Well, take a minute and think about your line at the beach…

When you fish from the pier or a boat you and your line are above the fish, usually straight down toward the bottom. But in surf fishing your line is out in front of you. As a result, you get a bend or sag in the line just like you would have when flying a kite.

Because of this bend, when a fish strikes it may be a second or two before you feel their tug. **To maximize your hooksets try this**:

Keep your line tight to your sinker at all times; always avoid slack line.

At the first sign of a bite reel down immediately and let your rod "load up" before setting the hook.

Use sharp, thin wire hooks and check them often to make sure they are at their sharpest. Don't waste money on "cheap" hooks; spend a few dollars to make certain that you have the best connection between yourself and the fish.

OTHER GEAR

Hemostats are also known as surgical clamps. Hemostats are used

to remove hooks from fish. They make it easier to reach down into the fish's throat and safely remove the hook. They can also be used to help hold and safely expel a bloodworm's pinchers. To retard rust be sure your hemostats are stainless steel, rinse them after use and store them dry.

Line clippers (fingernail) are best kept on a lanyard. They are used to cut and trim your knots, main lines and leaders.

Waist bait keeper is a plastic bait holder with a belt to attach

around your waist. This is the best place to keep your live bait fresh and handy.

Measuring tape is used to measure the size of your fish.

Sand crab traps can be found at your local tackle shop. Make sure the trap is well built and galvanized. Always rinse with fresh

water after each use.

Small zip top bags are used to carry various sizes of hooks, beads, swivels, grub tails and flies.

Disposable or digital camera is a must, because with catch and release, a camera is a quick way to document your record catch and preserve memories of incredible adventures.

Neck wallet or fanny pack is what I carry my gear in at the beach. If I'm fishing a sandy beach the neck wallet can hold plenty of gear. If I'm fishing the rocks or an area that requires heavier gear I'll use the fanny pack. Keeping equipment light and comfortable makes it a lot easier as you stroll the beach stalking the big one.

Knots
Improved Clinch

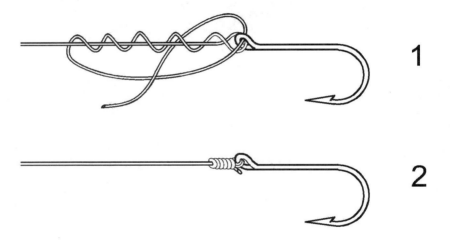

Snell Knott

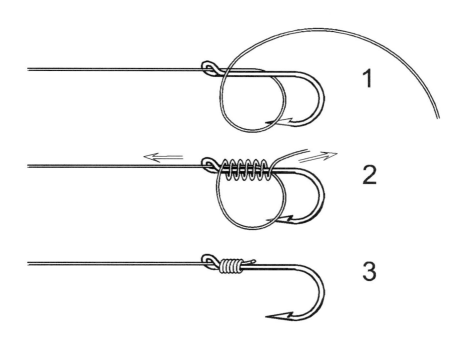

Dropper Loop

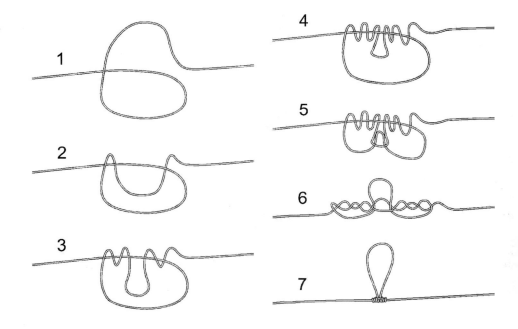

PalomarKnot

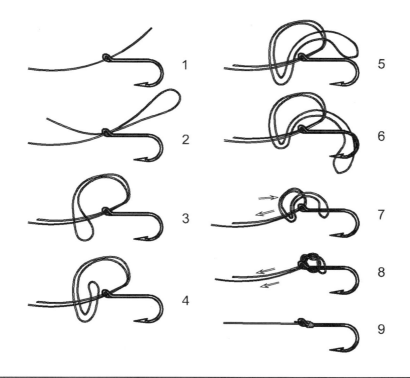

Uni to Uni Knot *(used to join lines and leaders)*

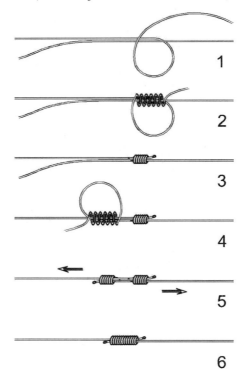

Blood Knot(used to join lines and leaders)

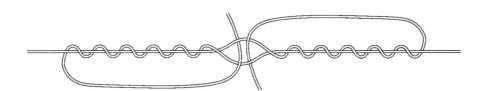

Surf Rigs

CAROLINA RIG

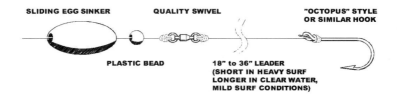

Application: Live baits, grub and fly. In larger surf use a shorter leader and more weight. Leader can be monofilament or straight fluorocarbon.

Tip*: Try a little variation; during winter I will use a very small orange bead above my hook and below the swivel. It slides on the leader just above the hook eye and grub and acts as an attractant to surfperch and yellowfin croaker.*

HALIBUT STINGER

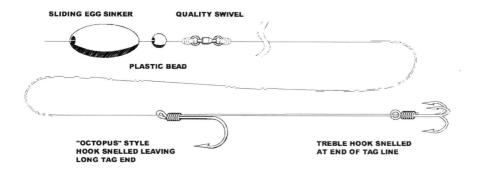

Application: Live or fresh-dead bait. Hook sardine, smelt, grunion or anchovy across the nose with the bait hook. Place the treble, barb deep, into one side of the bait's tail. Can also be used effectively with squid strips or whole fresh-dead squid.

SPLIT DROPPER LOOP / SPLIT SPIDER HITCH

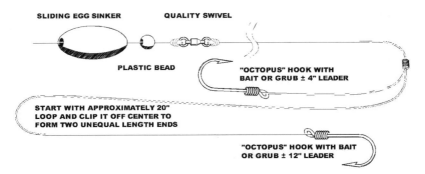

Application: Bait or Grub. Tie a dropper loop or spider hitch about 12" to 20" below the swivel and clip it so one tag end will finish at 4" and the other at 12". Tie a bait hook to the end of the short tag and a small treble hook to the long tag end. Attach a double loop leader to your mainline using the Carolina Rig, as illustrated above.

DOUBLE UNI CORBINA RIG

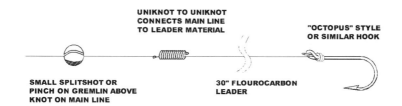

Application: This rig works great for targeting corbina. You may use it with a small pinch on weight or, for a more stealth presentation, with no weight at all. Fish the rig with a short cast and place your reel in free spool and allow your line to slowly flow off the reel as the bait is carried along the beach. Once your bait is sufficiently offshore put the reel in gear and be prepared to reel down on the first sign of a bite.

NOTES

CHAPTER 3

BAIT

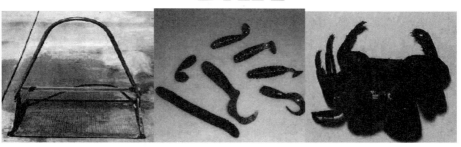

In This Chapter

**Types of Bait
Catching Bait
Keeping Bait Alive
Hooking various Baits
Freezing Bait
Artificial Baits**

Everything has a rule or two. Here's rule number one when it comes to which bait to use: Look for what occurs naturally around the area you are fishing. What's between the rocks or in the sand beneath your feet? Look around and see what you think the fish are eating. If you see mussels on the rocks or crabs in the sand you can be pretty sure that is what they're eating.

Sand Crabs *(Emerita analoga)*

When it comes to surf fishing, if I had to choose only one kind of bait, this would be it. Every surf fish, big or small, is continuously searching for one of the billions of soft-shell sand crabs. In spring, when the ocean warms to above 60 degrees, the sand crab emerges and sheds its first shell (molts). Much like a snake sheds its skin as it grows so does the sand crab. The sand crab's shell takes several days to harden after the molt. Almost completely defenseless the crab's soft-shell makes it easier for foragers to crush. During the warmer months sand crabs will molt frequently and grow rapidly. Throughout the summer soft shell crabs spawn and the odor emitted by the crab's bright orange eggs becomes irresistible to their hungry neighbors.

Catching Crabs

The best way to catch crabs is with a galvanized crab net. These nets can be purchased at your local tackle store. Make sure all parts are well galvanized and rinse thoroughly with fresh water after each use. These nets trap crabs against the galvanized netting as a wave recedes. Look for white or light gray crabs. Touch each suspect crab to see if it is soft and pliable. Some may be as soft as warm butter. Others will be more like bending a pop can. Because they tend to slide, the softer the crab the harder it is to keep on the hook. Crabs that are too hard will not be eaten. Crabs that are too soft will not remain on the hook. I've found that medium-soft crabs (those with a shell softness equal to pressing in a pop can) are the best bait.

Keep and transport your crabs in a waist bait bucket. A small piece of wet kelp helps to keep the temperature down and the bait fresh. If you plan to keep the crabs overnight cover them with some damp newspaper or kelp. Be sure not to crush them. I place the bucket in a cool dry place (the garage) and my wife appreciates that. By all means don't place them in salt water or refrigerate. Be sure to disturb them as little as possible or they will be cranky (and dead!) in the morning.

Two good times to catch crabs are on a large incoming high tide and at peak low tide. Peak high tide is going to be your most productive time. Time of day is not usually important unless there is excessive beach traffic that drives crabs down. When you first on the beach near the water, feel the sand with your bare feet. As you walk you'll notice that the sand varies from soft to firm as well as coarse to fine grain in different areas. Crabs prefer soft fine-grained sand that is easy to burrow into and rely upon it until their hard shell develops.

In most cases, crabs live in the soft sand just below the high tide mark. As the water passes over them they climb to the surface to feed. Softer crabs break loose and can be caught. Being soft, they find it more difficult to dig back in as the water recedes and are thus more vulnerable to predators and your crab net.

At peak low tide look for crabs to congregate in groups and become visible as the water recedes after each wave. Minus tide is a good time to look for these pockets of crabs that live on the outside sand bar.

Where To Find Crabs
Sand crabs can be found from British Columbia to the tip of Baja California. On beaches south of Santa Barbara we usually find them most abundant in the spring, summer and fall. When winter storm waves pound the beach and tons of sand are eroded and

deposited in bars offshore, the sand crabs go with it to ride out the storms. They return to the beach when the waves again re-deposit sand there.

The spring and summer seems to be the time when they are most available probably because these are their reproductive months. Females are larger than males with females producing as many as 45,000 eggs. Her distinct orange underside is a dead give away for both fisherman and surf fish. Sand crabs reproduce in their first year and have a lifespan up to three years.

To find crabs, start by looking near the waterline for groups of birds on the beach. Many local seabirds use their beak to probe the sand for crabs. Sand crabs like soft sand, they don't like rock or pebbly areas.

When you first arrive at the beach begin your search between the high tide mark and the ocean for signs of sand crabs. Look for moving water, receding from each wave. As a wave recedes look for little "Vs" in the sand. This is the characteristic ripple formed by a bed of crabs. Crabs feed for plankton on the incoming waves with extended feather-like antennae. With practice you will find that they are easy to see grouped in bunches and exposed as the water recedes between waves. The warmer the water, the closer they will be to the surface.

Sand crabs always swim, crawl and dig backwards. When a wave washes over them they can quickly relocate and dig back in leaving only their eyes and breathing antennules exposed. These are the appendages that reveal their location as the waves recede. They always settle in looking out to sea. You should approach them from above, on higher ground, to improve your chances of capturing them in numbers.

Look for patches of "Vs." Approach a patch and wait for the water to rush in over the area before standing on it. Once covered by water, step forward and place the net in the water and allow it to settle to the bottom. A surprise approach means crabs will be less likely to dig deeper into the sand and will be easier to catch. Continue as you "crab" to look up and down the beach to find more V-shaped clusters.

The most effective method of using the crab net involves digging sand into the net with one foot, or both feet alternating, as the water recedes. This breaks the crabs loose from the sand and yields larger catches. Incoming and outgoing waves can both be used for catching crabs, the latter being preferred. Always remember, water must be running *out* through the back of the net at all times or your content will swim, crawl, dig and disappear back into the sea in the blink of an eye.

Another good time to search for crabs is at a peak low tide— especially a minus tide. Crabs will congregate in groups on the outside sandbar that is concealed several feet below sea level at high tide.

Watch as the waves roll out for anomalies in the sand that looks like ripples on the surface of the sand. Dig here this is where you will find the crabs.

Over the years I've seen all kinds of contraptions to catch crabs. One guy even told me that a net was cheating because it made crabbing too easy. No matter what you use, even your hands, crabs are the best surf bait around. Your local tackle shop will carry galvanized crab nets for around $50.00

Tip: *Catch **hard-shell** sand crabs in the summer and freeze them for use during the winter. Save the larger crabs. When defrosted they will be just about as soft as a shell-less crab. Remember, don't freeze soft crabs or you'll have mush!*

Hooking Your Bait

Each type of bait has its own special way to be hooked. No matter what bait you are using the most important word to remember is "presentation." Most of all you want to make the fish believe that the bait is occurring naturally. It doesn't matter how good your bait is, if it's floating upside down or spinning wildly, it usually won't get a bite.

It's always good to practice before or and even after a trip on hooking baits properly. Don't wait until you are in the middle of a great bite to try to figure out how to hook your bait.

Sand crabs can be hooked two ways: from front to back or from back to front. They can also have the hook protrude from the top of their shell or from the bottom of their shell.

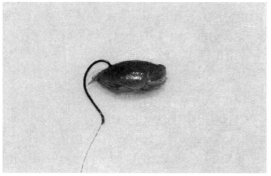

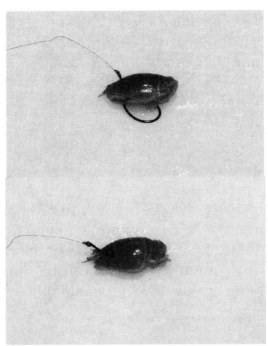

Three steps to hooking crabs (enlarged hook used for display)

Choose a sharp hook that best matches the size of the bait. I prefer to use split shot/drop shot hook or an offset octopus hook with a snell eye. I've found that using a snell knot creates a strong knot, good hook set and some elasticity. Octopus, mosquito and split shot hooks come in silver, black and red. Red seems to work well in the peak of summer when crabs are laden with bright red and orange eggs. Black hides well in bait and will quickly rust out of a fish that has been gut hooked.

For back to front: place the hook through the top "tail-end" of the crab and push it down and through. It should come out in the vicinity of the orange eggs. Pull the tip and barb through the crab leaving the eye of your hook exposed on the crab's back. Rotate the hook 180 degrees and bring it up through the underside, just below the crab's head. Be sure the hook end is sharp and protrudes just outside of the crab's shell right behind the eyes.

For front to back: place the hook through the top right behind the eyes of the crab and push it down and through. Pull the tip and barb through the crab leaving the eye of your hook exposed on the crab's back. Rotate the hook 180 degrees and bring it up through the "tallus" (which covers the eggs), on the underside. Be sure the hook point is sharp and protrudes just outside of the crab's shell.

Test how your bait rides in the water before you cast it out. It is better to see if it looks natural before presenting it to the fish. If it spins it will foul your line and will not catch fish.

Tip:
Corbina, croaker and perch all crush their bait. Always make sure your hook's point is exposed and the fish will do the rest.

Sometimes when a bite slows I'll flip the crab over and hook it with the opposite side up. This changes the "presentation" and might illicit a bite. Replace your sand crab when it has been partially eaten or after several casts with no bites.

Crab bed exposed at low tide

Sidewinder Rock Crabs (Pachygrapsus crassipes)

You see these guys scurrying across the rocks as you walk on to your favorite fishing jetty. The sidewinder crab has always been great surf bait in California. At times they may be a bigger challenge to catch than the fish. This rock crab is green and brown in color with lined markings on the back and legs. The larger crabs will have some purple marking as well. It possesses two respectable (and somewhat painful!) claws. They live between rocks in nooks, crannies and crevices.

The best place to find sidewinders is just above the waterline on rock jetties and in tide pool areas. Look for them between mussel clusters, in crevices or by flipping over small rocks. These crabs can be found at both low and high tide. Due to their keen eyesight, once they detect motion, they scurry off. When approaching, move slowly. Stop, look and see where they are positioned on the rock. Pick out a single crab (after some practice, a bunch of crabs) and as you approach watch carefully as to where that crab ends up. Take notice that they can run sideways very quickly; hence, why they are known as "sidewinders." Now that you've located the crab the best way to catch it is to pin it to the rock with your fingers. Get a grip and pull them from the rock to your waist bait bucket. Pinching hurts, so the best way to avoid that is to hold the crab by the back of its body pinching it between your thumb and forefinger. Start with one finger on top of the crab's back and one finger on the crab's underside. Hold him by the back with his claws forward. Some anglers prefer to hold them from both sides of the carapace (back shell) above the legs and behind the claws. You will need to decide what works best for you.

Another great place to collect crabs is in estuaries where rocks the size of shoeboxes line the banks. Pick an area and turn over the small rocks. Catch the scurrying sidewinders as they run off. In some areas these crabs will also live in mud burrows. By replacing the rocks after searching for crabs you will ensure that there will be even more the next time you return. Make sure the area where you collect your crabs is not a protected habitat area, so check for restrictions, as stiff fines may be your reward for not doing so.

Sidewinder crabs are very hardy and last quite a long time in the captivity of your garage. In fact, and I hate to admit it, when I was a kid, and ziptop bags were just introduced, one night while surf fishing I lost track of a bag of crabs. One week later, when I was surfing at the same spot, I found *the* bag of crabs. To my amazement the crabs were still alive.

Sidewinders, if kept in a cool plastic container with wet paper or burlap over them, will live for a solid week. Just enough time to slow their pinch down so you can get *"them"* on the hook without them getting you!

I place them in a vented, covered plastic container with a single mussel and a few small rocks. If they are going to be with me for a while I will open the mussel and they will feast on it. Each day, I rinse them in their container with a cup of salt water and they will stay fresh for some time.

Catching this crab can be difficult. Thankfully, hooking the crab is much easier. As with most baits match your hook size with the size of the bait. I use a thin wire split shot hook (or mosquito and octopus) size #1 or a #2 worm hook. A friend says you can never use too large a crab *or* hook when fishing them in the surf. He's also probably right—considering he holds several California State records!

There are two ways I like to hook sidewinders: My preferred technique is to hook the crab with a split shot hook directly through its abdominal flap (underside egg flap) and up through it's body. This also helps the bait to look natural and seems to work best when you're using larger (more painful!) crabs.

Match a thin wire hook to the size of your bait and insert it through the bottom back of the crab

*Pull hook all the way past the barb through the shell and your ready to fish*

The second technique has you start by grabbing the crab between your thumb and forefinger. Insert the sharp end of a worm hook into one of the crab's back leg sockets, through the crab's body, and exit the other side leg socket.

Remember that it is always important to use sharp hooks and make sure the business end of the hook is protruding through the shell, exposed to the barb.

Tip:
Sidewinders are one of the best know surf baits for catching big fish—especially perch! If you find an area where the surfperch are biting like crazy but you keep getting "dinks" go to the sidewinder. Only the biggest surfperch will eat them. But don't ask me; look in the record books—the last two record surfperch were caught on sidewinders!

Rock, Piling and Bay Mussel
Rock, Piling Mussel *(Mytilus carifornianus)*
Bay Mussel *(Mytilus edulis diegensis)*

Mussels are found anywhere you have substantial tidal movement, in conjunction with rock, pilings or jetty structure. More than anywhere else, mussels seem to thrive on pier pilings, docks, local jetties and inside wave-protected harbors.

Two different kinds of mussel work great for surf bait. One is common rock or piling mussel, which contains orange and brown meat. The other is the green bay mussel, which is full of bright chartreuse meat and can be found under small intertidal rocks.

The best time to collect mussels is at low tide. Rock and jetty mussel will be found in groups on rocks facing the open ocean.

Bay mussel is found inside harbor areas on the bottom of small rocks where only one or two may live.

Take only as many as you'll need. Although you may want to collect a few extra, shuck them from their shells and freeze them for later use. I divide them into small zip top bags and freeze them. Only thaw once. Mussels thawed and refrozen may become too mushy for bait.

Although it's nice to have fresh bait, I like to clean my mussels before going to the beach. When shucking mussel use a small knife to cut the tendons near the rear of the shell. On one side, near the back, there is a small indentation or hole. Insert your knife into this hole and slowly pull the knife forward toward the front of the shell. As you move along it will cut the tendon and once the shell is partly open you can pry it apart with your fingers.

Inside you will find two different bait textures: one very soft and pliable another very rubbery and strong. Both make good bait.

For hooking mussel, I'll wrap it around an octopus (seems ironic!), mosquito or split shot hook then pierce the rubber lip membrane last until it holds the bait in place below the barb. Be sure to puncture the lip membrane past the barb to

hold it securely. Some anglers also use dental floss or silk string to secure mussel to the hook.

Another hooking technique is to feed the mussel lip up the hook like a worm. I use the same technique seen below for blood and lugworms. "Feed" mussel up the hook to make it appear like a worm. If a bite takes off the bottom half of your bait just slide more down and poke the hook back through. (see: worm hooking)

Not unlike sidewinder crabs, mussel is very hardy and will last in a cool moist plastic tray for several days. They can be cleaned immediately or are a bit easier to shuck after being stored overnight. By all means, do not eat mussel that you collect. It's a filter organism that when feeding passes huge quantities of water through its membrane. It's "muscle" then retains and concentrates toxins it filters from the water including "Domotic Acid" the neurotoxin that causes amnesic shellfish poisoning which can be fatal.

Clams
Little Neck *(Protothaca staminea)*
California Cockle *(Clinocardium californiense)*
Pacific Razor *(Siliqua patula)*

There are several different types of clams that work well in the surf. My favorites include little neck clams, cockles and razor clams. Some of the largest spotfin croaker I've seen caught were those caught on fresh clam.

The best place to find clams (with the exception of Pismo) is in inlet areas that are flushed by daily tides. Most clams occur near or under rocks.

I look for areas that have small rocks (about the size of a shoe box) and turn them over. By using a small hand cultivator you can turn over the mud and sand near the rocks and find clams. I use gloves and the cultivator because of the many barnacles on the rocks and sharp objects in the sand.

The best tide to find clams is always low tide as this allows you to harvest in the area that is covered by water at high tide. As with collecting most types of bait, go down to your local harbor or inlet to explore and dig around at low tide. You will be amazed at what you find and you'll know exactly where to go when you next need bait.

When you're finished hunting the elusive clam replace the rocks and try to leave the spot as undisturbed as possible. Just take what you will need for a couple of days of fishing.

Clams will last in your refrigerator for a solid week. Be sure they are in a tight container. I open clams at the beach by crushing their shell with my pliers. You may also open them at home the night before. Be sure to keep them in their own juice so they don't dry out.

When you open clams you will find two distinct meats. One meat is very soft and should be put on the hook first. The other meat is very rubbery and is sometimes characterized by its bright orange color.

Now it's time to hook the clam. Once you've opened the clam carefully pull out all of the meat. First hook the soft part of the bait. Then hook the rubbery (sometimes orange) section. This will help the clam stay on your hook for a good cast.

This bait is very stable on the hook and is easy to cast. Check your bait periodically to make sure it's securely hooked. You'll find that clams are durable and attractive for surfperch, corbina, yellowfin and spotfin croaker.

Tip:
Clams seem to work their best in the months of October through December. As a clue to what fish are eating I look for beds of clams that form near the low tide mark in huge beds. You can usually find these in October and although they are not the clams we use for bait, it lets us know this is what the fish are eating.

Ghost Shrimp (*Neotrypaea californiensis*)

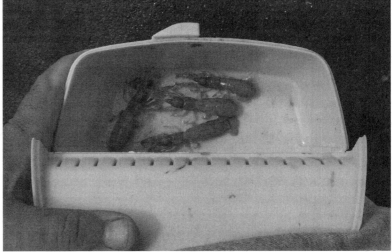

Ghost shrimp can be found in back bays, estuaries and many local tackle shops. Many people have asked me what fish like to eat these shrimp—the answer's always the same—whatever fish gets to them first!!

Ghost shrimp can be hand collected by using a suction pump (aka. "slurp gun"). Look for them at low tide in back bay areas that have moving water over mud and sand bars that are exposed at low tide. They live beneath holes they punch through the sand to feed and utilize as shelter. This is where to use your suction pump to pull them to the surface. To learn how to build a ghost shrimp pump refer to the appendix for plans and tips on using the pump.

If you don't have time to catch your own shrimp find a local tackle shop that carries them. The best size for bait would be shrimp the length of your middle finger or smaller. I like to keep my bait (either caught myself or purchased at the tackle store) in a small ice chest half filled with salt water.

I freeze half full bottles of water and place one twice per day into the ice chest. By keeping the bait cool, their metabolism seems to slow down considerably. The cool water also allows them to firm up and be much stronger and tougher baits. Shrimp kept this way can live as long as a week with regular replenishment of water and a cool environment. Some surf fishermen even place them in a small aquarium and place the aquarium inside a small refrigerator.

You may take them to the beach in either your waist bait bucket, plastic container or inside the small ice chest still filled with cool water.

Ghost shrimp are fragile and can be tricky to hook. Use a long shank worm hook for shrimp. Turn shrimp on its back and insert the hook near the shrimp's tail and "feed" the hook up through its body. Exit the business end of the hook, to just above the barb, just below the shrimp's head (through the carapace and between it legs). This method of hooking does two things. First, it allows the bait to lay flat on your hook. When the bait is flat it doesn't spin in the surf and looks most natural. Second, this helps to secure the bait to your hook and reduces the likelihood of the bait flying off during a cast. You'll have a lot better luck casting shrimp using this method and catch a lot more fish.

Once again, change your bait periodically, more often if you are not having success. Ghost shrimp work great for surfperch, yellowfin and spotfin croaker and corbina (In fact, it was the bait used for the current corbina world record) and just about any fish that get to it first!

Insert hook under tail

Feed hook up body

Exit hook through carapace and between legs

Live Worms
Bloodworms *(Glycera dibranchiata)*
Pacific Lugworms *(Abarenicola pacifica)*
Sandworms *(Nereis vexillosa)*
Pile Worms *(Neanthes succinea)*
Nuclear Worms *(genus Namalycastis)*
Innkeeper Worms *(Urechis caupo)*

Bloodworms and lugworms are two worm varieties that can be purchased at coastal tackle stores. Bloodworms along with sandworms and pileworms are segmented polychete worms of which approximately 700 species can be found along our coast. *(Your species may differ).*

Bloodworms are different from lugworms in several ways. Bloodworms are generally larger and have a stronger casing. They stay intact longer on the hook and can be used to catch several fish without changing the bait.

Lugworms are much less expensive but tend to disintegrate after one or two fish. All segmented annelid worms work great for surfperch, yellowfin croaker and corbina.

The technique used to hook worms is definitely an art and takes a bit of practice. When it comes to hooking blood or lugworms it takes practice to get the bait hooked just right. The first step is to entice the creature to extend its proboscis (mouth) from its tube lining. Inside the worm you'll find a set of four pinchers (two on lugworms). They appear as if they are tiny hooked claws. The worm uses these to catch its prey and to dig holes in the sand. On larger worms these claws can get your attention as they clamp onto your skin with a sharp pinch. The jaws are connected to poison glands that produce a neurotoxin that they use to subdue their prey.

It's essential to have the worm expose its mouth parts outside of the casing to hook it correctly. To avoid getting pinched I take my hemostats (i.e. stainless pliers) and pinch the worm's end to expose the pincers *or* rub the business end of the worm against my jacket to bring out the monster. The fresher the worm the faster and more pronounced the pincers and mouth.

To get the worm in a position to place on the hook I pinch (softly) the "neck" (below the mouth/pinchers) between my thumb and forefinger. Holding the worm firmly, insert the sharp hook end into the mouth (in the center of the pinchers). Slowly and carefully, trying not to puncture the worm casing, feed the worm up the hook. Pull the worm onto the hook until you reach the hook eye and mono knot. Firmly grasp the mouth and pull it over the hook eye. At this point the worm can also be slipped up the line. Leaving a one and one-half inch end, puncture the hook through the worm casing. Be sure to pull the hook past the barb so it sets well and will hold the worm in place as you cast.

Try not to get too much of the "blood" on you (your wife or girlfriend will appreciate it) and definitely avoid getting it into your eyes. The more fluid that remains inside the worm, the better it will attract the attention of fish.

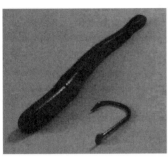

Hooking Worms
(plastic worm used for demonstration purposes)

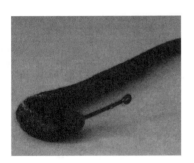
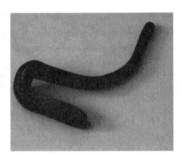

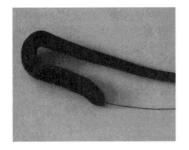
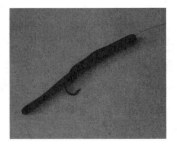

After a few bites, check your worm and see if you need to slide a new tail end down again. You can do this by retracting the hook from the worm casing, pulling the worm back off the hook, about one and one-half inch and then puncturing it back through the side casing. This again leaves a small tail dangling for presentation. Be sure to pull the business end of the hook through to the barb. With some practice you'll be able to catch more than one fish per bait. Leaving the bait in one piece not only makes it easier to use but also gives the worm a more realistic presentation and catches more fish.

If you find you are not getting bit put on a fresh one. Worms are only effective bait when alive. Once dead, discard them. Worms do not freeze and when dead emit an order that repels fish.

SANDWORMS *(Nereis vexillosa)*

Sand worms live beneath the sand and make great surf bait. Fresh worms work well for perch, croaker and an occasional halibut. These worms can be found at the beach throughout the year but are most active during spring and summer grunion runs. Their color reflects what they have eaten. Many times they are an olive green and orange from eating clams and other times they may be red and green from eating grunion eggs.

When looking for sand worms (this should be done at low tide) start by digging ten to twenty feet below the high tide mark. Most worms are down about 12"-36" and occasionally can be found in groups. Begin by digging a hole three feet wide and one foot deep.

Look for the worms as you dig. Remember, they can climb away fast, so keep a close eye. Catching worms takes a bit of practice--because they can dig away from you at a slithering fast pace. Start by grabbing the worm as it digs away. You may dig around it to catch the worm or pull it slowly backwards until it lets loose and comes out. If you pull too hard they will break off and you'll get only "half-a-bait".

Worms are very hardy and easy to keep. Simply place them in sealed plastic container and put the in the refrigerator. They will bunch up and stay lively for about a week. I like to use a #2 split shot hook and thread one or two worms, depending on size, up the hook for bait.

Nuclear Worms *(genus Namalycastis)*

These are monsters of worms. This is the worm you might imagine seeing in a science fiction movie. They are imported from the Mekong Delta in Vietnam and can be as much as six feet long.

They are harvested from the mud of the river and flown to the United States. They are collected from May through September and make a great summer bait.

They look a lot like a bloodworm but are much bigger. They will live for several weeks at room temperature (much like the warm humid temps of Indochina.)

It's best to keep them in a plastic container in the garage. Unlike most other baits, no refrigeration is required (Besides, who wants this thing rummaging through the leftovers?).

When using nuclear worms start by finding the tail. Cut a 6 " piece from the tail and begin by threading it up the hook. It's best to use a long-shank worm hook in these baits as it allows you to feed the worm up the hook and provide a realistic presentation. Be sure that the worm lies flat and the point of the hook is exposed to the fish.

Just as long as you keep the worm's head in tact it will live for many more days. Just progressively cut off pieces until you reach the head and then use that as your last bait. Remember to start at the tail. If you use the head first, the worm will die.

Since these worms are non-native and much larger than our local worms please do not release live specimens into the environment. There is much speculation as to whether these worms will survive in the cooler temperate local waters. Recent studies have shown that they may be able to adapt and it is always better to err on the side of caution.

Innkeeper Worms *(Urechis caupo)*

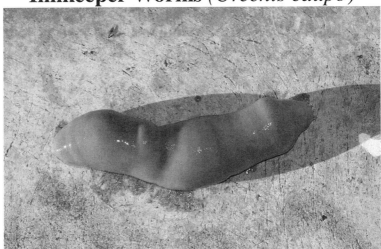

Innkeeper worms can be found in back bays and estuaries and work well for corbina and spotfin croaker. They live in sand and areas of soft mud where they burrow down and use their suction and filter motion to pump water that brings food into the slime net that they secrete.

Innkeepers are much less available than most surf baits and should be used sparingly. I try to use just a couple each year as they are very slow reproducers and can easily be fished out.

Finding innkeeper worms is very similar to finding buried clams or ghost shrimp. Innkeepers also live beneath a hole in the sand but have one distinct difference: Above their hole they produce a cone that seems to be nothing more than sand glued together by a mucus-like secretion. I have also found many of these worms in the shade under docks, bridges and other shade producing objects.

Once you find these holes and "volcanoes" use the same suction method as for ghost shrimp. The worm looks much like a hot dog and is about the same size. Once caught put it in a cool shaded area as you look for more bait. These baits can only be kept for a few days and do well in the refrigerator and ice chest.

There are a couple of ways to prepare and hook innkeeper worms. You can fish them intact for larger fish or strip them into several baits by slicing them lengthwise.

Tip: *Soak a handful of lug worms in an inch of milk and within 24 hours they will double in size. Yum!*

Keeping Bait Alive and Fresh
Sand crabs, sidewinders, and mussel
Keep your live bait in a shallow plastic container with a small piece of kelp adjacent to the bait. The container should be kept in a cool dry place (like your garage) and disturbed as little as possible. Keep moist but ***do not*** immerse in salt water. Sand crabs will live for two to three days. Sidewinders and mussel will stay alive and fresh for up to seven days. Mussels can also be kept in a damp burlap sack.

Bloodworms, Lugworms, and Ghost Shrimp
Keep these refrigerated but **do not freeze**. Undisturbed bait will live for two to seven days in your refrigerator. When undisturbed, lug worms will live up to fourteen days; or about twice as long as bloodworms and ghost shrimp. Place bags or boxes of bait in a brown paper bag. When returning from fishing put bait in the refrigerator as soon as possible. When worms die put them in the trash. Once again, dead worms are no good because they excrete an odor when dead that does not attract fish.

Freezing Bait

Being prepared by freezing bait a day or week before a fishing trip can make the difference between catching fish or merely practicing your casting techniques.

Each package should contain enough for one day's fishing. I place mussel and pre-cut strips of squid together and freeze in a small snack-size zip top bag. Frozen squid and mussel become tougher after freezing and are easier than fresh to keep on the hook.

When the fishing day is over and you won't be going back to the beach tomorrow, toss your leftover worms in the trash. Worms cannot be frozen.

Sand crabs, sidewinders and ghost shrimp should all be frozen separately in small one-day size packages. Ghost shrimp tend to get mushy so freeze them as soon as you get back from fishing.

Place bait packages in labeled brown paper bags in the freezer. Don't be surprised if your wife or girl friend finds them and throws them out. To avoid this, it might be a good idea to invest in your own "bait freezer" for the garage! ***Once per year throw out old bait and start over.***

Carrying Bait on the Beach

I use a waist bait bucket which keeps my bait handy and within reach. These buckets work well for holding bait at the beach, during transport and for storage between trips. Be sure to rinse any empty bait containers in clear fresh water when you come home to ensure they will be ready and safe for the next batch of bait. (Few things are quite as repulsive as a bad day of fishing or a malodorous bait container!)

A final word about how to best present your bait in the surf. Here are a few rules I like to follow:

1. Make sure that your bait is correctly positioned upon the hook so it does not spin. Check your bait frequently and adjust it when necessary
2. Match your bait in both size and color to what is currently living in the area you fish. This will be the natural forage. If the crabs in the area are green and brown or the clams orange and red, try those colors
3. Fan cast: cast straight, cast right and cast to the left at multiple angles to cover the largest area as you search for fish
4. Use the sharpest thin wire black hook possible. Always be sure you are using the sharpest hook possible. I said that twice because it's soooooo important!
5. After casting out, always be sure to keep your line tight to your sinker by reeling up any slack. This will help you to feel the bite and catch more fish. It will also help prevent your line from fouling in the surf.
6. Once you've cast out, try reeling the bait in slowly using a stop and start motion with your reel. Vary the speed of your retrieval. When using lures try a very fast and slow retrieval speed as well.
7. You will always catch more fish if your line is tight and straight in front of you. If there is a long-shore current pulling your line up or down the beach try this technique: Cast your bait up into the current and let the drift push your bait down the beach. As your bait moves down the beach walk along to keep the line in front of you. Once the bait comes too close to shore, reel in, walk up the beach and repeat. Be aware that fish will frequently be foraging in the inshore trough that may be just a few feet in front of you. Don't give up on your retrieval until you see your bait on the sand in front of you.

8. If, after fan casting an area you don't find fish move down the beach. I usually move about 100 yards, observing the water as I go for indications of fish, structure or eddy currents. I try fan casting and moving until I find biting fish. Remember, fish move frequently and many congregate in schools to feed; you will need to move too for improved success.
9. Check your main line and leader frequently for damage that may occur from contact with rocks or structure as well as the abrasion that catching fish produces. Also inspect your knots after catching a large fish. There is nothing more disappointing than hooking into the fish of a lifetime only to loose it due to a line or knot failure.

10. Be continuously observant about exactly what you were doing when the fish took your bait. How far out, what angle, speed of retrieve, any currents present, is there a trough, sandbar or structure, color of water, etc. By treating every outing as a learning experience you are certain to become a more proficient angler while all the while increasing your enjoyment.

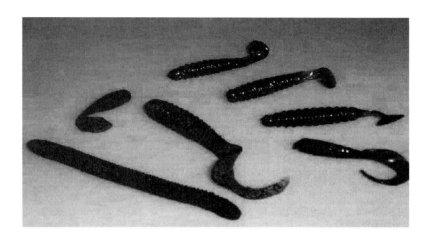

Artificial Baits:
Grubs
Flies
Lures

Artificial baits come in many shapes, sizes, materials and colors. *Remember rule number one: always match your bait to what occurs naturally in the area you are fishing.* But also, don't be surprised if something that seems unnatural for the area works too. Look for lures that are similar in shape and color. Opt for darker lures if you're not sure of the exact color--darker trout-sized lures (those designed to catch trout, not imitate them) are useful because they cast an enticing shadow to fish in almost any light situation.

Although there are many artificial lures, those most commonly used in local waters include grubs, spoons and flies.

Grubs and flies can be used year round but seem to work best during winter months when the water is colder and bait is scarce. Spoons seem to work best during the summer months when the water is warmer and fish are chasing anchovies, sardines, smelt, grunion and fry in the surf.

Grubs are nothing more than a small plastic worm. Their color attracts fish and their tail entices them to bite. The most productive size of grub is two inches. Remember to match the grub size to local bait. If you fish with a larger size and get no bites go to a smaller grub. Grubs generally have three common tails: straight, curly and stumped (A.K.A. swim or paddle-tail).

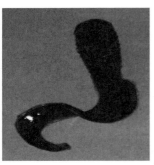 *Curly*  *Stump/Swim*

Curly and stumped tails give the lure more action and seem most productive in daylight hours. Straight tail is much like a short worm and seems to work best after dark. Stump tails produce the greatest amount of vibration when retrieved that may add attraction after dark as well.

Use different grub colors depending on the color of the water you are fishing. If you throw the wrong color you might as well be dragging a spark plug out there. With waves crashing and locally churned murkiness, most surf fishing areas have cloudy water. Whites and muted colors cannot be seen and won't work. Dark colors, which cast a more enticing shadow, match surrounding bait and work best. Motor oil, red flake, gray flake and brown seem to do the job.

TIP: *The most productive grub colors are: Smoke with glitter, motor oil glitter, watermelon/chartreuse, pearl green/silver glitter, sour grape/purple, caterpillar/yellow and green, avocado, green pumpkin, green/pearl and pumpkin with black flake* **(and all colors which mimic the color of bait that naturally occurs in the local environment)**

Hooking the grub is very similar to stringing a bloodworm—with one big exception-NO pinchers! First, place the hook against the outside of the grub to get an idea of where the hook's point end will punch through the grub body. Begin by pushing the sharp hook end into the very middle of the grub's head.

Check the grub to see if the grub has lines, like a seam, left by the mold. If so, be sure to center your penetration between these lines. Holding the grub between thumb and forefinger feed the hook down toward the tail and exit with the sharp end. Once most of the shaft is buried in the plastic grub, stop. Carefully, pull the grub head back toward the hook eye. This will even-out the grub and help to flatten it onto the hook. Again, think about presentation. The more the grub looks like it's flat and freely moving through the water (without a hook!) the better chance you'll get a bite. Check your grub every other cast (every cast if you get a bite) to be sure it's flat and tracking best through the water. Do this by pulling the grub back and forth in front of you to see how it tracks through the water. It's shaped to swim naturally and should look that way.

 *Hold the hook next to the grub to see where the hook will exit the bait*

 *Begin threading the hook through the middle of the grub toward the tail*

 *Finish by exiting and pulling the grub straight onto the hook*

The Carolina Rig is the most common rigging for fishing grubs in the surf. In larger surf or strong current a shorter leader is best because it helps to keep your bait near the bottom. As with all surf baits it is important to be in contact with the bottom at all times.

Tip: (*Hot sauce tip #2*)*When fishing the grub (just like with an unfrozen sand crab) cover it with hot sauce from your local taco stand--you'll be amazed how well it works! Reapply after several casts. (I hear you laughing!)*

Flies

Flies are still somewhat of a mystery to me. By far my most effective fly has been the Clauser Minnow, a two-eyed minnow shaped fly about two inches long. My favorite colors are off white with motor oil green. As with all hooks, make sure your fly hook is sharp.

The best way to rig the fly on a spinning rod is to use the smallest sliding egg sinker (one-quarter to one-half ounce) and a twenty-four inch six pound test leader. The Clauser is effective for surfperch, halibut, striped bass and corbina. Fish the fly in the same manner as with the grub. Slowly retrieving your rig along the bottom will help keep the weight in contact with the sand. This can provide added attraction as the weight kicks up a plume of sand as your fly dances along behind. Unlike worm fishing, use a long leader to help keep your fly up off the bottom. Some anglers apply a "floatant" which comes in gel and spray forms to increase the buoyancy of the fly.

For those that practice the fine art of traditional fly fishing a suggested minimum is a 9-foot, 6-weight rod with a sinking weight forward line. A standard leader is in the 4-foot range with a 1X tippet. An open mesh line-stripping basket is useful to keep yourself from tangling your line in the swash while fighting the fish in the waves. Do not use a closed bucket style-stripping container as a wave may catch you off balance.

You must be highly aware of "beachgoer traffic" as the majority of people that come to the beach are not fishermen and most have no clue what a backcast is.

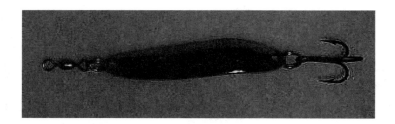

Lures

A wide variety of lures work well in the surf. The most important rule to using lures effectively is to know what baits fish eat, when (what time of year) they occur and what they look like. Fish don't get big by being stupid. Try to think the same way a fish does. What does the bait around me look like? If fish are eating clams and mussel their food is black, brown and orange---shouldn't my lures be that color too?

Here are a few examples: Let's say you're fishing in the surf for halibut and there has just been a grunion run. Wouldn't bait that looks like (color, shape and size) a tasty grunion probably work best? The answer is yes!

On another day you are fishing for corbina and you know they like sand crabs. Wouldn't it be smart to use a lure that looks like a crab and has some of a sand crab's coloration like the orange roe found beneath its tail? Or a flashy lure that looks like a small baitfish they may eat. Remember to look around you and see what occurs on the rocks, sand and water around you. This is what the fish are eating. If you match your lures to these natural baits you'll have the best chance of landing a whopper.

Krocodile®, Kastmaster® and Needlefish® all work well with a slow retrieval. In Mexico, Krocodile® lures are used as large as two ounces. But in our local surf the smaller one-half ounce model is the best size. Where as grubs are most productive in winter months, lures like spoons are most productive in the summer. Halibut often mistake this shiny lure for wounded bait in the days following a grunion run.

My recommendations: Krocodiles® in 1/8th to 1 ounce, KastMasters® in 1/8th to 3/4th ounce, Needlefish® in 1/8th to ½ ounce. For hard swim baits I use Lucky Craft® Flash Minnow 110, or Rapalla® MaxRap sinking or suspended baits.

CHAPTER 4

Fish Of The Surf

In This Chapter

Types of Surf Fish
Strikes
Best Baits
Best Spots
Rig Up

Our fourth chapter serves as an introduction to the fish that live in the California surf.

California Corbina (*Menticirrhus undulatus*)

Pound for pound corbina are the best fighting fish in the California surf. Their color is a silver-gray with a white belly. Their body is elongated and there are narrow wavy diagonal lines on the sides. This croaker has a single fleshy projection called a barbell, on the lower jaw. The caudal fin (tail) is unusual in that the upper half has a concave trailing edge, the lower portion is convex. Their body is very dense providing stability in shallow surf.

A strong and aggressive fish, the corbina will often strike bait on the run. Some of their favorite meals include mussels, clams and bloodworms, but their main diet consists of sand crabs. Corbina feed in shallow water by running their sensitive chin barbell across the bottom to search for sand crabs, clams, worms and shrimp.

These fish frequently forage in just inches of water and beachgoers are often surprised when one swims between their legs. They use the incoming tide and wave motion to search for sand crabs. In just inches of water, they prowl suspended in the inshore trough waiting for their chance to charge the beach as surf rushes ashore.

Corbina live from Santa Barbara to Cabo San Lucas. On a recent trip to Mexico's East Cape I learned first-hand that Baja has some of the best croaker fishing in the world. Go diving in the East Cape and you'll see hundreds of schooling croaker swim beneath you creating a huge carpet across the ocean floor.

Another great place to get a look at these fish is from your local pier during an incoming tide. It's not uncommon to see four or five at times, just inches away from swimmers!

Although most corbina are found near shore they have been caught in nearly eighty feet of water. Marine biologists believe corbina can grow to about thirty-two inches. A twelve-inch corbina is roughly three years old. A twenty-inch fish weighing roughly four pounds is about nine years old.

During winter (November through April) corbina migrate away from the beach and move into deeper water while others will move into local estuaries. Corbina will spawn from May through September, with the majority of the activity, taking place around mid June to Mid August. During this time they are everywhere in the surf.

The largest corbina feed on the largest soft-shelled sand crabs. These crabs are most numerous during the warm water months of July, August and September. Sand crabs must "molt" or shed their exoskeleton, as they grow larger. The crabs are vulnerable and apparently quite delicious at this stage. They grow faster and molt more frequently in the warmer waters of summer. Corbina rarely run in large schools and are usually found alone or with perhaps no more than two other fish, working the crab beds.

STRIKE: Very distinctive--they inhale the bait and immediately swim away. Rather than a nibble, like with surfperch, the corbina picks up the bait, straightens the line and quickly swims away. There is no question when there is a corbina on the other end!

Corbina Tip: *During the summer focus your fishing on flatter, gradual sloping beaches on a rising tide*

BEST SPOT: Inshore, twenty feet from the dry sand in the inshore trough. Sometimes corbina may also be found a bit farther out near the wave impact zone where another trough has formed. Flatter, more gradual sloping beaches with fine grained sand, are best. Corbina can be found in as little as six inches of water.

During the summer, corbina feed often during incoming low to high tide periods. They can be seen "surfing the swash and sliding the beach" as successive waves fill in over the high tide sand crab beds.

In winter, you'll find corbina in back water areas such as harbors, bays and estuaries. Try ghost shrimp, clams or innkeeper worms. This is the natural forage they are feeding on in the inner waters.

BEST BAIT:
Live Bait:
Soft shell sand crab, ghost shrimp, clams, mussel, lugworms and bloodworms

Artificial Bait: Plastic grubs, Kastmaster ®, Krocodile®, Clauser Minnow, crab and shrimp imitator flies

RIG UP: (Carolina Rig, see chap. 2) One quarter, to as much as, a one ounce sliding egg sinker, bead, swivel, eighteen to thirty inch 6 pound test fluorocarbon leader and a number two to six (depending on the size of bait) split shot/drop shot, octopus or mosquito hook.

Yellowfin Croaker (*Umbrina roncador*)

Not unlike other croaker (corbina, seabass) yellowfin also have a distinctive goatee barbell. Shiny gray and silver in color they are more rounded and flat like barred surfperch. The are often white on the belly, yet they have very distinctive yellow fins on the top (dorsal), and bottom (anal fin), and tail (caudal fin). Larger yellowfin commonly have green, blue, and brown oblique stripes.

Yellowfin croaker can be caught from Ventura to the tip of Baja. They usually stay in water shallower than twenty-five feet (although they have been caught in more than sixty feet) and congregate in medium to large schools. Although they can be found in inches of water some of our best bites have been in deeper water near the outside trough created beneath the outside surf impact zone.

The yellowfin are very aggressive feeders, perhaps due to heavy competition among large schools of fish. Their strike is surprisingly strong. Not unlike corbina, yellowfin spawn from

May to September. They can be caught all year long along the coast. Some of your best, and at times wide open bites, will be just following their spawn in late summer.

The yellowfin grows to about twenty inches. A fish this size would be about ten years old. One half that size is about four years old.

STRIKE: When a yellowfin picks up your bait you know it! One of the strongest strikes for the size of fish--they will usually pick up your bait with a strong nibble and swim away immediately.

BEST SPOTS: Unlike corbina, yellowfin croaker are schooling fish and are sometimes found in massive schools of one-thousand or more. They are found close to shore in the surf lines and trough. They also frequent waters outside the surf line in debts up to sixty feet.

In late summer yellowfin will school in large numbers to chase small baitfish like anchovy, smelt and grunion. They will also feed en masse, grazing the bottom for worms, clams and shrimp. These schools consist of like sized fish that are voracious eaters. It's not uncommon to catch as many as one per minute when they go into a crazed post-spawn frenzy!

BEST BAIT:
Live Bait: Sand crabs, ghost shrimp, clams, bloodworms and mussel all work well.

Artificial Bait: lures such as small spoons, spinners, hard baits and plastic grubs will also do the job.

RIG UP: Most yellowfin croaker weigh in the one pound to three-pound range. The Carolina Rig, using a small egg sinker, works best for bait and grub applications. For lures like spoons and spinners, use a direct mono knot. The ganion grub rig is also productive when the bite is very hot.

Barred Surfperch (*Amphistichus argenteus*)

The first word in the name "surf" perch tells us a lot about this pugnacious little fish. With two rows of teeth it is well known as a forager. One set of teeth allows it to catch and the other to crush a variety of baits. In fact, not unlike the barred sand bass, surfperch can also pick up small clams and encased worms and conveniently crush their shells to reach their soft interior; they do so while surfing the waves back and forth in the shallow inshore break.

The barred surfperch is characterized by a set of brassy vertical bars, alternating with vertical spots, all outlined in light green stripes. Occasionally, in the colder water years, and on beaches above San Francisco you may catch the Red Tail Surfperch with its distinctive red fins set upon the unmistakable surfperch shape.

Because barred surfperch enjoy a variety of water temperatures they can be found from Canada to the tip of Baja. Surfperch migrate from shallow water to deep water in mid summer looking for a cool spot to rest. In fall they move into the shallows to feed and remain active in the surf through winter and spring. Their spawning habit is unusual in that they give live birth. Surfperch mating takes place in the late fall into winter; a great time to catch the largest fish. Gestation is around 5 months so the young are released in spring to early summer. If you happen to catch a female carrying young please treat her gently and release her promptly.

Surfperch can be caught in as little as two inches of water. Like yellowfin croaker, perch also roam in schools but do not generally range far distances. Barred surfperch grow to roughly seventeen inches and about four pounds. Females grow quicker than males with a twelve inch fish being about five years old.

BEST SPOT: On open beaches, barred surfperch live in the inshore trough moving in and out with the surge of surf. The churning action dredges up clams, crabs and worms. They are very close to shore usually within sixty feet or less. Surfperch will often frequent rip currents, jetty eddies and channel edges. Many fish are caught in less than four inches of water!

Huge perch can also be found near jetties, pilings and rocky points. Fish rely on rocks for shelter and for the food that comes from the mussel and crab that live on the structure. Big perch get that way by finding shelter and food and by not getting caught or eaten. They do this by backing into the crevices of underwater rocks.

So next time you fish from the rocks try downsizing your sinker (as light as possible) and drop your bait straight down right in front of you where the sand meets rock. Let your bait swing in and out with the current, keep the slack out of your line and hold on. The big one's waiting there just for you!

BEST BAIT:

Live Bait:
Surfperch eat sand crabs, mussel, clams, ghost shrimp, lug worms, bloodworms and sidewinder crabs

Artificial Bait:
Hard baits (Rapalla/Lucky Craft Lures), plastic grubs, and flies such as the *Clauser Minnow*.

During wintertime, when food is scarce, surfperch are very aggressive toward the small plastic grub. Also, during this time perch eat the sidewinder crabs that are washed off the rocks. Some of the largest perch I've ever seen (and the CA state record) have been caught on this bait.

In late spring and early summer, surfperch are more widely disbursed and prefer natural bait. Not unlike most inshore surf fish they love soft shell sand crabs.

Tip:

When you find areas with biting small perch try this: Switch to sidewinder crabs. Only the largest perch will eat these—as witnessed by the enviable fact that both of the last state record perch were caught on one!

STRIKE: As mentioned earlier, the surfperch, with its two sets of teeth, is a food grinder. The bite is normally a series of nibbles followed by a strong pull. Because surfperch inhale and exhale their food it is best to set the hook following the first set of nibbles.

RIG UP: Once again the Carolina Rig (sliding rig) works well for both bait and grubs. In small surf, go without a sliding weight and try a tiny pinch-on weight (like a split shot or Gremlin). For lures and hard baits tie directly to monofilament. Fish for surfperch on two to six pound, pink or red monofilament.

Walleye Surfperch (*Hyperprosopon argenteum*)

Walleye surfperch are easily distinguished from other Southern California surfperch. Silver in color, they have larger than average eyes, blue accents at the top of their back and black tipped tail and ventral fins.

Their upturned mouth may be the reason for their feisty nibble. Scientists have found these fish in as deep as six hundred feet of water, although most are caught in the shallow waters of the inshore trough.

Because they congregate in schools they may be concentrated in one area. Although you will rarely find one larger then eight to ten inches, once in a while you'll catch one that's a hefty twelve inches and about six years old. Walleye, like barred surfperch, can be found on sandy beaches and rocky shores near jetties, piers and landings.

BEST SPOT: Walleye surfperch congregate in schools. One of the best spots is in the shallows of the inshore trough where fish forage for worms, clams and sand crabs to be churned in the current. Another good area is near rocks and pier piling structure. Walleye surfperch prefer to live in areas with clean moving water especially around shore surf, pier pilings and rock outcroppings.

BEST BAIT:
Live Bait:
Sand crabs, sidewinder crabs, lug and bloodworms, mussel, clam, ghost shrimp and almost any other surf food you can find.

As with all fish, perch prefer the bait that occurs naturally throughout their territory. Perch found on sandy beaches will prefer bloodworms and sand crabs from April through September. Perch found around rocks and pilings will prefer mussel and sidewinder crab. *Always look for the bait that best matches what the fish are currently eating*—It's probably in the sand or clinging to the rocks around you.

Artificial Bait:
When bait is scarce in winter and the water turns colder, perch love the plastic grub. Rig the grub using the same sliding rig. Remember when the surf is bigger, or there is a strong side current, use a heavier sinker and a shorter leader. When the conditions are calm use a lighter sinker and a longer leader. In both cases keep in

mind that if you want to get bit, your grub must keep in constant contact with the bottom.

Perch also like hard baits, spoons and flies like the Clauser Minnow.

STRIKE: Walleye, like all perch, are nibblers. They move quickly onto bait as it is churned in the tidal zone. But unlike corbina or croaker they do not immediately swim away with the bait. They prefer to inhale and exhale the bait using rows of teeth in their mouth and pharyngeal plate to crush food before swallowing. The exception to this may be in winter when food is scarce and they tend to chew less and swallow more.

Most often, the larger the fish the more fierce the strike. Many times, especially in spring, when they are spawning, schools of small fish will nibble and pick your hook clean. But don't be surprised if a much bigger fish hears the commotion and bites. Most walleye surfperch weigh less than one pound, but an occasional "kicker slab" may put a smile on your face!

RIG UP: Again, the Carolina rig will work best in the surf. Your leader should be shorter in strong surf or side current (12 inches) and longer (18-24 inches) in calm waters. Both will insure that your bait stays in contact with the bottom. Use a light one-half ounce sliding sinker in calm conditions and up to an ounce sinker in surging surf.

Leader and main line in either red or pink monofilament in two to six pound test. Walleye also like to strike the small silver Kastmaster® and other small spoon jigs.

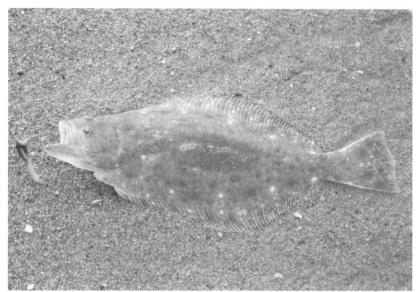

California Halibut (*Paralichthys californicus*)

The California halibut's most distinguishing characteristic is a pair of eyes on the dark side of the fish. One side of the fish is brown and lightly spotted. The other side, blind by nature, is white. Unlike other flatfish (flounders, sand dabs, etc.) halibut have a row of *very sharp* teeth. Most California halibut are caught between Morro Bay, to the north, and Cabo San Lucas to the south.

Primarily burying themselves in the sand except for their eyes, they love to lay-in-wait for their prey. Most halibut dwell in five feet to two-hundred feet of water. Halibut, like other fish, come into the shallows to feed and spawn. With some exceptions, halibut migrate near shore during spring and summer.

In the dead of winter, when prey is scarce and fish are less active, they are usually found in deeper water.

California halibut grow to more than five feet in length. A keeper at twenty-two inches is about five years old. The current

California all tackle record (as of the date of publication) is 58 pounds 9 ounces, caught at Santa Rosa Island. They have a life span of about 30 years. The older and larger fish (between thirty and fifty pounds) are breeding stock and can rear more young in one year than a fifteen pound fish can in three years. As such, they are a very valuable resource and should always be released. By far the best eating halibut are those between twenty-two and thirty inches in length (six through twelve pounds).

BEST SPOT: Halibut live where sand meets structure. They will roam near structure where the baitfish they eat seek forage and shelter. With the exception of spawning times, these fish usually congregate where they find food. Near rocky structure area they can be found on the leading edge where sand meets rock.

During grunion runs, halibut can be found just off the beach in very shallow water as they track the bait into their spawn area. In the summer months, especially when water is warm, they congregate in shallow water as they chase bait fish like anchovy, smelt, sardine and grunion.

In early spring halibut move in close to shore to spawn. This is the best time to catch these fish at the entrance to local estuaries like the Goleta, Santa Clara and Santa Ana rivermouths, Los Alamitos Bay, Mission Bay and well inside the Long Beach Federal Breakwater. In the dead of winter, halibut move to deeper water and are infrequent visitors along the beach.

Santa Ana Rivermouth

BEST BAIT:
Live Bait:
Although halibut have been taken on bloodworms, their favorite foods would include smelt, anchovy, grunion and sardine. Live and fresh dead work well. After casting, retrieve your bait slowly, always keeping in contact with the bottom.

Artificial Baits:
Recently, I witnessed a twelve pound halibut taken with the *Clauser Minnow fly*. These realistic bait imitations along with two to four inch grubs and swim tail plastics, also work well. Not long ago I landed a twenty-two inch halibut on a one and one-half inch motor oil grub -- a real departure from the norm. The best colors for grubs and swim baits have been motor oil, olive green with silver fleck, cinnamon with red fleck and other dark colors. Silver spoons such as the Kastmaster® and Krocodiles® also work well.

In most cases look for colors that represent the colors of bait they would eat naturally. For open beaches and rocky areas try hard baits like Lucky Craft® and Rapala ® lures with a varied retrieve.

STRIKE: Halibut rarely hit bait and run. Covered with sand and stuck like glue to the ocean floor they usually bite and hold onto their prey. Slowly they ingest the bait using their very sharp rows of teeth to rake it to pieces. Halibut, unlike other fish such as tuna and yellowtail, may prefer their food dead and will usually crush it before ingesting.

Halibut may be one of the hardest fish to hook. One reason is the placement of their mouth. Unlike other fish, their mouth opens to the side and the hook slips out missing the roof or floor. Many anglers use a "trap" rig which utilizes a small treble hook or "stinger" hook tied three inches below their main bait hook. If you do use a trap rig be sure to use a non nickel plated hook so that it can rust out quickly if it needs to be left in the fish.

RIG UP: When using a grub or live bait, the sliding Carolina Rig works best. Remember to keep the leader short on days with strong waves and currents and longer on calm days. Leaders from twelve to thirty-six inches are best. Tackle up with heavier leader material to reduce the chance of being bitten off. Eight to twelve pound leader is ideal. When fishing around rocky areas, rod size can also be increased along with line test. I like a 7' to 9' rod matched with 12 pound test line.

If you wish to use a "trap rig," tie the "stinger" treble hook three inches from the main bait hook. This can be accomplished by tying a short leader to the eye of the main hook or by leaving an extra long tag line after snelling a hook (I like this best, even when fishing in the boat, because there is one less knot to tie and worry about).

Make sure the "stinger" treble is small and bury at least one of its hook arms into the tail of the bait. This will not only hide the hook but will also help the bait to remain straight and give a more lifelike presentation.

Cast this bait and retrieve it slowly across the bottom. Be aware that the bait needs to be kept in contact with the bottom at all times--so in this case, it's better to use more weight then less.

Tip:
Hey, I've just touched the surface of halibut fishing. Check out chapter 5, Surf Fishing Techniques for California Halibut, *it's all about fishing for trophy butts in the surf.*

Spotfin Croaker *(Roncador stearnsii)*

The spotfin croaker has a distinct black spot at the base of the pectoral fin and can have bluish-gray or brassy on their sides with a white belly. Males during spawning season can be mostly copper

in color, while females may develop a black streak on
's.

Spotfins are found in as little as 4" of water and as deep as 60 feet. Most are found from Santa Barbara to the tip of Baja. Some traditionally notable areas for good spotfin fishing include Emma Woods State Beach, Huntington Beach, San Onofre and Gurrero Negro Baja California.

Local spotfin range from 12"–30" in length. A 27" inch fish is about 15 years old. The state record is currently 14lbs but fish to 20lbs have been reportedly caught from the Pacific Coast beaches of Baja.

BEST SPOT: Spotfin croaker can be found in estuaries, harbors and the open ocean. Although they can be found inside back bay areas all year they tend to swim into the open ocean during Spring and Summer to forage on sand crabs in the intertidal zone.

During winter, spotfin croaker find home in the tranquility and relative calm and warmth of harbors, back bays and estuaries. This is where they find shelter from storms and forage that lives here.

As spring rolls around spotfin move through the tributary channels and entrances into the open ocean. Throughout the summer they rove the beach looking for sand crabs and worms exposed by the surf. Occasionally, tucking back into the bays for shelter, food and spawning.

BEST BAIT:
Live Bait: Sand crabs, mussel, clam, sidewinder crab and ghost shrimp. Seasonally the best bait for winter would be clams and

sidewinder crabs. For the remainder of the year I would prefer sand crabs and mussel. It's always good to have a variety of baits to try because you never know what food the fish are keying in on.

Artificial Bait: I have seen some huge spotfin caught on Krocodile and Kastmaster lures. Fish these jigs in the 5/8 to 1oz size. They also hit hard baits, swim baits and I have even landed a few on motoroil grubs.

STRIKE: Spotfin, not unlike corbina, have an accordion lip that they use to suck food like worms, ghost shrimp and sand crabs up from the bottom. They rarely nibble on a bait. Spotfin prefer to inhale a bait and swim off. Many times their bite is nothing more than a strong pull on the other side of the line. There is no mistaking when they have taken your bait and hurriedly swim away to their next meal.

I prefer to let them pick up the bait and then reel down on the line until the rod loads up with their weight. It is then that I set the hook and continue with constant pressure until the fish is up on the sand.

RIG UP: When fishing live bait the best setup would again be the Carolina Rig. Spotfin are not as wary as the corbina and don't require such a stealth offering. Unless fishing from the rocks your rod and reel should be 6' to 8' and matched with a spinning reel loaded with 4 or 6 pound mono. Often these fish can get as large as 10 pounds and frequently will make an initial long run; then put up a reasonably stubborn fight, until the end.

On rock out croppings like jetties I like to upsize my rod and reel with a bit longer rod and 6 or 8 pound test. Fluorocarbon leader material seems to work the best because it is abrasion resistant (good when fishing around rocks) and difficult for the fish to see at higher tests.

When fishing artificial baits like Lucky Craft® and Rapala® hard baits and spoons tie them directly to your main line. When fishing grubs use the Carolina Rig with a longer leader in calm conditions and shorter in big surf and along rocky areas.

Tip:
Spotfin feed in the sand and mud so remember to keep your bait in touch with the bottom. Match your baits to what occurs in the area and remember that these fish swim in large schools so when you find one there may be many others waiting to be caught!

Other Fish In The Surf

Surfsmelt (*Hypomesus pretiosus*)
Jacksmelt (Atherinopis californianiensis)
Sargo (Anisotremus davidsonii)
Striped Bass (*Morone saxatilis*)
Round Stingray (Urobatis halleri)
Thornback "Banjo" Shark (*Platyrhinoidis triseriata*)
Shovelnose Guitarfish (*Rhinobatos productus*)
Leopard Shark (*Triakis semifasciata*)
Grey Smooth-hound Shark (Mustelus californicus)
California Grunion (*Leuresthes tenuis*)
And many more…

CHAPTER 5

Surf Fishing Techniques For California Halibut

In This Chapter

Best Places to Find Halibut
Time and Tide
Halibut Surf Tackle
Surf Rigging
Lures and Bait

I'm asked all the time, "what's the best tasting fish from the surf." Well the truth is, I release all of my fish back into the water with one exception—the occasional legal halibut.

It would appear that I'm not alone.

The California State Fish and Game Department has stepped up their monitoring of halibut fishing this year in response to concerns about over fishing. Due in part, as the result of so many anglers turning to halibut because of the closure of salmon fishing along the West Coast.

Fortunately, halibut fishing has been exceptional this year from San Francisco Bay to the Mexican border with three fish limits the rule. Recent reports seem to tell us that the halibut population appears to be rebounding from the years when gillnets ensnared them in obscene numbers before being banned to within 3 miles of shore.

A non-migratory fish, the California halibut grows to over 60 pounds with the record 58lb 9oz fish caught at Santa Rosa Island. These fish live in a depth range between 2 and 200 feet. In the winter most halibut swim into deeper water to feed and take refuge from winter storms. In the spring, summer and fall halibut come into much shallower water in both the surf and just offshore, to feed and spawn. A "legal" halibut is one measuring over 22 inches and is one of the most sought after catches in the surf.

Best Places to Find Halibut

Boat fishermen love to target halibut but fishing for them from the surf can also be productive. Some of my favorite places to fish for halibut are along the open beach, around jetties and near estuaries and river mouths.

Open beaches offer a challenge when looking to target halibut. When you arrive at the beach find a high spot near the water's edge and look up and down the beach for signs of fish. Because surf fish congregate near areas of jumbled or foaming water look for small rip currents that form plumes of off-colored water just off shore. Another area to target is offshore structure including holes, kelp beds and reefs. Once you spot these areas, cast your bait or lure along the edge of a rip current, structure or where rocks meet sand; This is where fish will be waiting to ambush bait.

Halibut also congregate in the offshore troughs that are formed by wave action as the sand is deposited in shallow bars. These troughs are easiest to find at low tide and run parallel to the beach. One trough will form outside where the waves break farthest out from the beach (at low tide), another trough will form where the waves break (during high tide) near the shore. Cast over and drag your bait through these troughs to entice halibut to bite. Fan casting at various angles will allow you to cover the greatest area including the inshore trough.

Open beaches that have a rocky point adjacent to them are also great areas to target fish. Find where the sand meets the rocks and fish along this edge. Halibut commonly lie-in-wait along these edges.

Jetties also offer some great opportunities to catch halibut. The California coast is littered with man made and natural jetties that provide structure and habitat, bait fish and feeding halibut. As with open-beach fishing, it's always smart to cast along the edge of rock where it meets sand to find the fish. But there are some subtle differences to also look for when fishing along a jetty.

When approaching the base of the jetty, where it meets the sand, look out to sea and take note of the direction of approaching waves and swells. If the waves are approaching the jetty from the right, a natural eddy will be generated on the jetty's opposite side (left side). If waves are coming from the left, an eddy will form on the jetty's right side.

Eddys are much like a rip current and are characterized by swirling, foaming off-colored water. Fish congregate in an eddy where moving water churns up bait and allows them to stay hidden while they wait to ambush food. Once you find the eddy, fish along its edges and cast through the middle to find the fish. Don't be surprised when the tide or swell direction changes and the opposite side of the jetty becomes the best place to fish.

Estuaries and river mouths are almost always connected with a channel for fish to run from warmer breeding grounds out into open-ocean. The California coast was once blessed with hundreds of natural estuaries that acted as rookeries for growing fish stocks. After unprecedented development and growth many of these breeding grounds were filled or closed off to ocean circulation. Still there remain a few in almost every beach community that offer fantastic opportunity for surf fishing.

When approaching an estuary or river mouth area use the same rule of observation as with jetties—determine the direction of the swell and tidal current and how it effects water movement. Unlike with jetties, tide flow will have a much greater effect on fishing the river mouth. A high going to a low tide will pull water out of the estuary and toward the open ocean. A low going to a high tide will push water and waves up into the estuary and change the direction and movement of fish.

Again, look for the formation of eddys. On an incoming tide, an eddy may form just inside the river mouth. As tides recede, an eddy may form just outside the river mouth in an area of open-ocean. This is where the fish will congregate to lay in wait for your bait. Fish your bait along this edge and allow it to be pulled by the tide and current into the strike zone. Try to stay away from areas where the water is moving too quickly as fish here will not be willing to chase your bait.

Fish will normally be reluctant to expend excessive energy to pursue bait in a heavy current, preferring to utilize slack water and eddies to lay-in-wait for a morsel of food to drift past.

The best way to become familiar with good fishing areas is by looking up your favorite strip of coast at: http://earth.google.com/ and mapping out a strategy for fishing. At this site you'll be able to zoom into any coastline on the planet and find the best spots to fish. Look for areas where jetties and river mouths meet the beach. You can also find areas where there are large inshore holes or sand bars, points, kelp and reefs. Google® has stated they plan to update maps every two months so be aware that the conditions may at times be different than depicted on the internet. Take some time to research your areas and you'll have a lot more luck with a lot less gas!

Time and Tide

Each beach will have it's own special time where fishing is best but here's a general guideline that you can follow. When fishing the open beach, halibut fishing seems to be best at or near low tide. Lower tides give you the advantage to wade into the surf and cast well beyond the surf line. Low tides also allow you to reach the outside holes and structure that hold fish. Although some spots do fish well at high tide, our best luck on the open beach has come at peak low minus tides and the first push of incoming tide.

Near jetties I've found the best tides to be medium to high tide where the halibut come in close to the rocks to feed and spawn. Watch for high and low astronomical tides (the greatest swings in tidal movement because of moon phase), which move more water and create a larger eddy circulation. These tides improve jetty fishing and really stir the water up for halibut. If fishing the rocks at low tide, try using the jetty as a platform for casting to areas outside the rocks that don't usually get fished.

Estuaries that are connected to the open ocean by a series of jetties or a river have always been very productive. Because fish use these river inlets to enter and exit the estuary there is no better place to target big fish. Strong currents during incoming and outgoing tidal flows sometimes makes it almost impossible to fish for halibut in these rivers.

That's why fishing just minutes before, during and after low tide and high tide will give you your best chance at catching a keeper. Halibut are characteristically ambush predators lying-in-wait either partially or entirely concealed beneath the bottom sand or gravel. They will occasionally actively pursue bait and lures but prefer to wait for food to come to them. During *slack tide periods* your bait is presented in a more natural manner giving halibut a better chance to attack your bait.

One more tip: A premier time to fish for halibut is during and just after the grunion run. As grunion move ashore to spawn on the beach halibut capitalize on the opportunity and move into the surf line to feed. A good year for grunion runs will hold halibut near shore for the entire season as they search for bait, spawn and digest what they have found. Runs typically occur every two weeks in spring through summer, one or two days after the new and full moon phases. Check local regulations on open season for collecting grunion. It is usually closed April and May to protect the fish during peak spawn. (Also the best time to fish the halibut chasing them). During open season it is legal to capture grunion, **only by hand,** and pin them on as bait. Some anglers like to "butt hook" them and cast them out so they swim away from shore. If you capture enough to freeze some grunion for later use be aware that using a dead grunion as bait during closed season may get you a ticket from DFG.

You'll find a tide graph in real-time and a schedule of grunion runs at www.fishthesurf.com.

Tackle

When it comes to tackle you have a couple of different choices of rod and reel combinations depending on whether you will be using live bait or lures.

For fishing lures it's good to get started with an 8' rod rated for 8-16lb line. Spinning and conventional reels both work well. For lure fishing, I prefer a conventional reel because it seems better matched to my rod when it comes to fighting the fish and directing it away from snags. There are many good conventional reels on the market so just make sure you have a smooth casting reel with at least 300 yards of 8-12lb line.

Conversely, when it comes to live bait I like to use a spinning reel because it seems easier to cast with a set up that includes a long leader and sinker. Once again I like to use a longer 7-9' rod rated 8-16lb test and a 3000 size-spinning reel rated for 300 yards of 8lb test monofilament. I also recommend a spinning outfit for lures when you're fishing in a tight area like under a bridge or near a pier or anywhere casting is restricted.

Rigging

When it comes to halibut rigging I use two basic setups. The first is the Carolina rig which works best with bait (and also has some lure applications). The second rig is a lure tied directly to my monofilament.

Carolina rigging consists of a sliding egg sinker, bead, swivel, 18"-36" leader and a hook. In small surf a ½ ounce egg sinker works well. In bigger surf or when fishing in the wind use a 1-ounce or heavier sinker to keep my bait on the bottom.

I like to use a black swivel, a clear bead and a fluorocarbon leader. In *small* surf my leader may be as long as 36". In *large* surf always use a shorter leader (12"-18) to be sure your bait stays in constant contact with the bottom.

The hook I like to tie to the end of my leader is a conventional "j" hook, which is very sharp and made of thin black wire. The most important part of the rig is the hook so be sure your hooks are new, in good condition and very sharp. Some good hook choices include split shot, mosquito and octopus hooks in sizes 1, 2 and 4.

The Carolina rig works best with all live and fresh dead baits and also with a fly tied to the end of the leader in place of a hook.

The second setup I use when fishing with lures is either a straight connection of the lure to my mono or using a uni to uni knot to connect my main line to 10lb fluorocarbon leader and then tying on my lure.

Fluorocarbon leader is a good idea whenever I'm fishing near rocks or over structure. Fluorocarbon allows me to use a heavier leader and it's much more abrasion resistant than monofilament and less visible to fish.

So in open beach areas I'll tie directly to mono; while in rocky areas like jettys and reefs, I'll always use the fluorocarbon leader because of its abrasion resistant qualities.

Lures and Bait

When it comes to lures and bait fishing for halibut the options are almost endless. It seems that almost everyday I see someone on the Internet or an email that lets me know that something we never thought would work *is working*. As a testament to this, over the last two years there has been a great crossover of freshwater lures, especially bass lures, which work well in the surf.

Baits that Crank

Without question the most productive surf lures have been both Lucky Craft® LC 110 (now FM 110) Sardines and Rapalla® SXR-10 Slash Baits. These lures are best cast out and retrieved with a stop and go motion. They should be tied straight to your main line or onto a short uni to uni connected fluorocarbon leader. Most halibut move slowly so a fast retrieve may pass the fish by. A fish attractant applied to your lures will also help to attract fish and make them hold on once they bite.

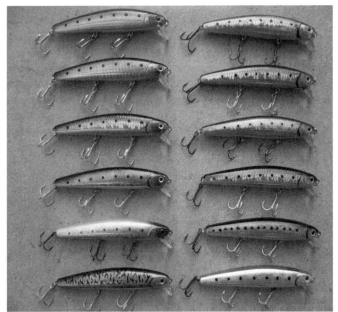

I highly recommend you wash these lures in fresh water after each trip to the beach. When you see dull hook tips or rust replace the treble hooks and split rings.

Both of these lures seem to work best and look most natural during slack tides when you can use a stop and go motion and the lure is not fighting the current.

Spoons
The two most effective spoons for the surf have always been Luhr-Jensen's silver Krocodile® and the Acme Kastmaster®. These lures are easy to use and should be tied directly to your line. A good size to use is one between 5/8oz and 1oz. Some recommended colors are chrome, chrome and mackerel pattern, chrome and blue and prism Krocodiles®.

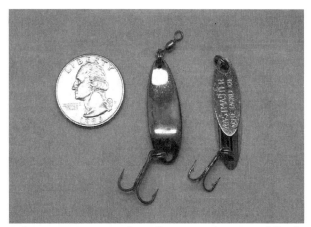

A long fan casting pattern and a slow retrieve, with the lure bouncing across the bottom, seems the most effective presentation. Fishing spoon lures at peak low tide will allow you to cast outside the surf line to offshore structure and holes. Or, fish these lures at high tide and you can concentrate on the inshore trough where halibut hunt for food.

Plastics

Grubs and plastic lures also work great in both the open beach and near rocks for halibut. Two styles of plastics seem to work best in the surf.

The first, known as a grub, is in the shape of a pollywog. Most grubs in the 1 ½" to 3" range seem to work best. Attach grubs to your line using the Carolina Rig. Be sure to use a short leader in big surf and a longer leader in small surf. Grubs work best when cast out in a fan pattern and retrieved slowly, using stop and go motion, across the bottom. Be sure to use enough weight, as directed by the surf, surge and wind, to keep you bait in constant contact with the bottom. Always remember to use a sharp thin wire hook and maintain tension in your line so you can feel the strike and react instantly.

Unlike the grub, *plastic swim baits* can be tied directly to your mainline. Use a leadhead that matches the size of your bait and the current you will be fishing in. Once again remember to keep your bait in contact with the bottom and don't be shy from dunking your plastics in "hot sauce" to attract and catch more fish.

The best bait colors for halibut have always been the colors that reflect what the fish have been eating. Sardine, anchovy, grunion, smelt green, brown and oranges have always worked along with stark white that probably resembles squid that halibut scoop up from the bottom. Some of our most productive colors include: dark blue or black back, electric blue side stripes and clear or silver/gray and prism sparkle belly. I like to use 4" swimbaits that imitate grunion on a $1/4^{th}$ or 1/2 ounce jighead. Also, try varying bait sizes to try to "match the hatch."

<u>Twitch Baits</u>
Twitch baits are made of the same material as plastic baits but require different rigging. These baits are a true crossover from fresh water bass fishing and have become very effective when used in the surf for halibut. Look in your local tackle shop for Basstrix and Sluggo products.

Rig the twitch bait with either a small $1/8^{th}$ leadhead (or the new Mustad "Power Lock" weighted hook) and tie it directly to your line. You may also rig it using the drop shot method.

The drop shot rig is simply a sinker on the very bottom of your line and a loop 12" – 24" up your line for the hook and bait. When using the drop shot rig, don't tie the lure directly to your dropper loop. Run the line through the hook's eye and allow the lure to slide freely on the loop in your line. This will give the bait a much more natural look, impart erratic action and help you to entice more fish to bite.

Twitch baits work best when they are cast out and retrieved slowly using stop and go then twitch motion. When using the drop shot rig try to find the *lightest sinker* you can use and still stay on the bottom. This will help to reduce the number of snags and tangles in the rocks. Look for lure colors that reflect what the fish are eating and fell free to use the "hot sauce" on these baits too.

Surf Fly

Fly-fishing has always been productive in the surf. But the skill, equipment and work needed to be productive using a fly outfit has kept most anglers from picking up the fly rod and heading down to the sand.

By using a fly presented on the Carolina Rig it is easy to use both spinning and conventional reels. The most effective surf fly is the Clauser Minnow that mimics a small grunion or smelt in the surf. Lime, olive green, red and white and chartreuse with white have always been productive colors. Apply "hot sauce" to the fly and fan cast the bait past the surf line. Using a slow retrieval, pull the fly across the bottom in areas near structure and rocky outcroppings.

For those with the skill and patience for a fly rod; a 6 to 8 weight rod with a weight forward sinking tip line seems to work very well. A line basket will also save you a lot of headache by keeping your line from fouling in the swash of the waves. Again a fluorocarbon leader secured to the end of your fly line will give both abrasion resistance and stealth capabilities to your presentation.

Live Baits in the Surf
There are many types of live bait locally available for use when targeting halibut in the surf. Live, fresh dead or unfrozen sardine, anchovy, smelt and grunion all work well in the surf. Additionally, strip mussel lip, threaded on the hook like a worm, is natural bait for halibut and also seems to work well when the bite is tough.

Use either a spinning or conventional outfit and the Carolina Rig. I like to hook my baits (anchovy, sardine, smelt, grunion) through the bottom and top lip with my hook to be sure they swim correctly and give the most natural presentation. Fishing with natural baits (like the grunion below) requires a much slower retrieval and periods of stop and start that allow the lazy halibut to catch up with their next meal.

Both anchovy and sardines can be purchased at your local tackle shop or quality fish market. Smelt and grunion can be caught by anglers and kept alive or fresh dead for bait. You'll find smelt near docks, inlets and inside local harbors. They can be caught with a bait catching rig or with breadcrumbs. Grunion can only be caught by hand during a grunion run at your local beach—but be careful, as there are specific times they are not allowed to be collected.

With so many choices for bait and halibut rigging it's almost hard to know where to start. Take a moment to ponder my tips and don't be shy to ask a friend about their "secret flattie" techniques. It's with information like this that you'll be able to formulate your own style and teach the rest of us how it's done.

So when it comes back to the answer of which fish from the surf I like to eat it'll always be the halibut. Once in a while I'll take one in the 24"-30" range and have a delicious meal. The rest I'll let go to fight and grow big for another day. So take some of the tips from what you've read today and add your own ideas—*That way you'll be guaranteed to discover the best technique to catch halibut at your favorite beach.*

CHAPTER 6

Taking Control

In This Chapter

**Fighting the Fish
Fishing in the Wind
Fishing in the Current**

Fighting The Fish

Fighting a large fish on the beach, with surf and surging water, is like nothing you've ever done before.

Most fish hooked from the surf don't head straight out. Rather, they tend to swim parallel to the beach. Surf fish move up and down the beach using the swell and surge to their advantage.

The best way to fight fish in shore beak conditions is to first back up, once you're hooked up, and use the rise on the beach for leverage.

Always keep your line taught with a bend in the rod. A longer tapered "medium action" rod allows for your pole to "load up" and give you more control over the fish.

Pull the fish toward you using the incoming waves (as you do with a rising and falling boat). Slow or stop retrieving completely when the waves are rushing out. If the outgoing surge is particularly strong walk back toward the water giving line while still keeping tension on the fish. As the fish reaches the shallows (two feet of water or in the inshore trough) move forward toward the water always keeping your line taught and the rod bent.

As you move closer to the water remain focused keeping a wary eye on the size and timing of the shore break. Nothing is worse than losing sight of the next wave and becoming its next victim. *Always know were you are in relation to the surf.* Use the shore break to bring the fish closer to you and not you closer to the fish.

Once the fish is in the very shallows (about one foot of water) stop reeling and slowly walk back up the beach dragging the fish with you. If you encounter an exceptionally strong "swash" (backwash current as the wave recedes) or you are battling a large fish, you may have to retreat again toward the ocean. You might find that you need to play the fish back and forth until it is tired enough to come up onto the sand.

With larger fish, the "yin and yang" of landing your catch is a real test of patience and finesse. Fighting fish from the beach is a challenge but with experience you'll develop a feel for it and know when the time is right to move toward and away from the foaming water. With practice you'll get good at landing your catch on the beach and be surprised by the size of fish the receding water leaves behind.

Fishing in the Wind (The Great Equalizer)

Fish really have an edge when it comes to the wind. Onshore or long-shore winds make it more difficult to feel bites and react to them. Wind also requires a heavier sinker to cast, to keep your bait down and to keep it in contact with the bottom.

With light test line you want to be tight with the bottom so you can feel bites and bottom structure. Lighter lines also have a tendency to stretch more and make it more difficult to get a good hookset. To be successful with surf fishing you must always have you line tight to your sinker.

When it's windy a bow appears in your line and delays your strike detection as the fish picks up your bait. In turn, it also delays your hookset movement from reaching the point of your hook and the fish.

The best way to fish wind swept conditions is to keep your line taught by casting straight into the wind. After casting, keep your line low to the sand to reduce wind resistance. Do not fish up sand unless you're hooked up and want to use the leverage provided by the rise. Keep low to the water to avoid having your line "ballooning" in the wind.

Remember, constant retrieval of your line is essential to keeping the line taught and feeling the bites. Always use more weight in these applications (as much as 1oz) to make sure your bait remains in constant contact with the bottom.

It also helps to pull your line and bait in the direction the wind is blowing. Many times the drift (caused by waves and wind) is too strong for fish to catch up with your bait. In these cases, cast into the wind and walk slowly along the beach keeping your line in front of you as it drifts along.

Unlike onshore winds, winds blowing offshore are ideal and have little effect on fishing technique. In addition, they provide better visibility for the fisherman. Offshore winds help to "clean up" the ocean surface and make the water clearer. Some of my best surf fishing days have been during fall and California's infamous Santa Ana winds.

FISHING IN THE CURRENT

Finding current can many times mean finding the fish too.

Strong long-shore currents may make it difficult to fish but water movement created by rip currents, jetties and beach structure attract fish because they provide ideal feeding conditions.

Your first step is to find the rip currents and eddies by looking for rippled, off-colored and foaming water. Most fish will be darting in and out of the clear water (looking for food) that surrounds the current breaks.

Fish the edge where off-color or "dirty" meets clear water. Using a slow retrieve, try bringing your bait from one side of the off-colored plume to the other *and* along its edges.

Pay special attention to the direction of the current and cast your line above the eddy and allow it to be dragged by the current into the strike zone. Check your bait often and recast into the current to allow your bait to work itself back though the moving water.

Most eddies will form on the opposite side of where the waves are making contact with rock and structure. Eddies will form an area of circulation that will create a concentration of food along with slack water that the fish will utilize. Cast along the edges of that current to find fish.

When fishing rip currents on the beach, know that they may form for just a few minutes and then dissipate. When this happens continue down the beach to find another disturbance that may form just as quickly as the last rip left. At other times a rip current may persist for quite a while and create a defined channel that can be productive for several hours.

The critical factor is for you to be observant of the conditions that you are presented with and to capitalize on the opportunity to target the fish that use these currents to their advantage and to thrive.

CHAPTER 7

Tide And Moon

In This Chapter

**What Causes Tides
What Tide Is Best For Surf Fishing
How To Read Tide Charts
Tides And Time Of Day
The Moon's Affect On Surf Fishing**

Tidal movement and moon phase are two of the least understood natural phenomenon yet combined they have one of the most pronounced influences on surf fishing. Higher tides expose more food and provide more underwater structure than low tides. Full moon phases give fish more light to feed and can dramatically change the hours of day found to be the most productive.

What Causes Tides

It is important to understand the relationship of tidal fluctuations and moon phases because of their pronounced affect on the quality of fishing. Tidal theory includes the interaction between gravitational and centrifugal forces.

The levels of the ocean fluctuate daily as the Sun, Moon and Earth interact. The Earth's inward pull, known as gravity, affects the Moon by holding it in orbit. The Moon's gravity, at the same time, is also pulling at the Earth. The gravitational attraction of the Moon causes the oceans to bulge out in the direction toward the Moon, (sub-lunar point). The Earth itself is also being pulled toward the Moon (and away from the water on the far side). This creates another bulge on the opposite side of the Earth away from the Moon, (antipodal point). The combined gravitational forces as the Moon orbits around the Earth and as both, together, revolve around the Sun, causes the world's oceans to rise and fall. With the Earth rotating on its axis while all this is happening two tidal cycles occur each day, (in most places). Variations in coastline topography can have significant affects on localized tides.

The gravitational force of the Sun upon the Earth is approximately 46 percent that of the Moon. This makes the Moon the single most important factor influencing tides. The period of the Moon's orbit around the Earth is approximately 27.3 days "sidereal". The period of the Moon's phases in relation to the Sun is approximately 29.5

days "synodic" (a "Month?"). The effect is that in each 24 hour day the "apparent" moon shift is 13 degrees to the east in relation to the Sun and stars. This is why the tides are ever shifting and change by about 50 minutes each day. Besides the abnormal flooding and nuisance they cause they also have a dramatic effect on fishing.

In the following sections we will learn which tides are best for surf fishing and how to read tide charts.

What Tide Is Best For Surf Fishing?
(There are really two times...)

The optimal tide would allow for roughly a six-foot tidal swing. For example, a morning low tide of 0.2 feet and an afternoon high tide of 6.2 feet would allow for this six foot swing. Tidal movements greater than this creates strong upcoming and receding water movement. These excessive movements make it difficult for fish to see and catch bait. Tidal movement less than four feet, and especially during diurnal or neap (small swing) tides, cause the opposite condition: very little water movement and thus much less rotation of bait through the strike zone.

In most circumstances (see below), the best time to surf fish is on an upcoming high tide. Two hours before through two hours after the high tide. *I like to fish for corbina and spotfin on the incoming tide because each successive wave moves them farther up the beach and over the sand crab beds. For surf perch I like fishing the high tide going to low tide as it seems the receding waves and water help to pull my bait into the offshore trough where the fish are.*

When fishing during the slack high tide periods (the time exactly when peak high tide is reached) water movement is at a minimum and many times the bite will fade away and then become dramatically active again as water begins to turn, receding on the low tide cycle.

There is an exception to this rule when fishing for halibut, near rocks and from undredged beaches. At these times fishing at peak low tide and peak high tide may be essential.

A good case in point would be for halibut which seem naturally lazy and love to bury themselves in the sand and wait for bait to pass by. They are most active at both peak high and low tide. This is when tidal current is slowest and they have to work the least to eat.

Also, when fishing areas that are rocky (or adjacent to rock, rivermouths and natural beaches) many of the most favorable areas may not be accessible until the tide drops. Try your favorite spots at both high and low tides to find when and where the best places to fish are. You may be surprised to find the best structure can only be reached at the lowest tide.

Tip:
The largest tidal changes are during the full and new moon phase. This will cause the largest movement of water and provide both opportunity and challenge to the fisherman. Some of the best fishing and bait catching conditions occur during these moon phases.

How To Read Tide Charts
Tide charts can be found at your local tackle store, surf shop or on the world wide web. They come in small pocket sized books or in the form of a graphic calendar. I prefer tides presented in graph

form as seen in the following illustrations. This format makes it very easy to visualize the changes in tidal movement and thus plan your trip accordingly.

Below are graphic calendar illustrations of tidal movement. One of the first things you'll notice using a graph is that the best fishing tides occur roughly every two weeks.

Semi-diurnal tides (The Best Fishing Tide)

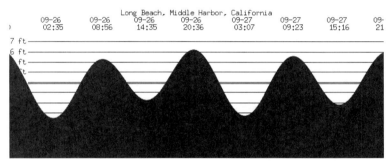

Large water movement

Diurnal (neap) tides (The Least Desirable Tide)

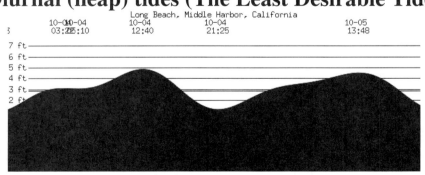

Very little water movement

Tides And Time Of Day

Unlike other species we fish for (especially the white seabass) the time of day for surf fishing is not as important. If I had a preference I would always want to fish at sunrise and sunset.

Why? Because baits cast an enticing shadow and look their most natural in the soft light of sunrise and sunset. Some surf fish are less wary, feeling less vulnerable in low-light conditions. But many surf fish, and especially the corbina, have very little interest in the time of day. Some of my best catches have been in mid morning to early afternoon. But with that said, the time of day is important when combined with the "people factor".

There is no doubt that the "people factor" comes in to play when fishing the beach. In the summer time, when the beach is most crowded, loads of little feet pound the sand and the stomping and splashing frightens fish. At these times I do fish early morning and at sunset when the water is calm and the fish come close inshore to feed. At times when I must fish during "people factor" conditions I seek out and fish only the areas that are least crowded. This helps to avoid the finicky fish and the agitated parent who assumes I'll hook their kid.

Over the years I've really noticed that areas with people in the water have far fewer fish. A good idea is to find fishing locations that are the farthest from convenient parking and you'll have a much better chance of catching fish.

TIP:
The best time to surf fish is when the tidal movement has at least a six foot swing, on an upcoming high tide, two hours before until two hours after peak high tide and in the evening or morning when the "people factor" is not a factor.

The Moon's Affect On Surf Fishing

There is much speculation about how the Moon affects fishing. Many long-range fishermen swear by the notion that a full moon means a great bluefin tuna bite. But this is mostly a myth with very little scientific backing.

One thing we do know about the moon phase is that during a full moon fish will feed at night because they are able to see and track bait. During new moon periods (when the moon is dark) fish feed most actively in the very early morning and evening when the light is bright enough to see their forage but low enough to hide them as predator.

During a full moon period the biological clock for fish is pushed back while they digest what they have caught and eaten during last night's full moon. Morning fishing during these periods may well prove unproductive.

TIP:
Full moon nights mean surf fishing may be better in the afternoon and into the night.

CHAPTER 8

Catch And Release Surf Fishing Etiquette

Diminishing fish stocks is a big worry for every fisherman. Unfortunately, improper management of the resource and toxic urban runoff, have dramatically decreased the size and number of fish. By all means, it is acceptable to keep fish should you want them for the dinner table. Just try to release the ones that you don't—that way they'll be there again and again when you come back fishing another day.

Always check the DFG regulations for "health advisories" regarding consumption of certain species of fish from designated areas. There are toxins in our coastal environment that are persistent in the fish that will cause serious illness.

Catch and Release

> *"Game fish are too valuable to only be caught once."*
> *Lee Wulff*

Here are a few ideas on the best way to release fish:
Anglers catching fish to be released are urged to use methods that minimize the damage to the fish. Here are a few tested tips that will help you with the release process:

A. Wet your hands before touching the fish

B. Avoid grabbing and handling the fish body

C. Don't handle your fish by wrapping them in a towel

D. Avoid letting the fish hit the boat deck, rail or falling in to the sand

E. If possible, keep fish in the water when removing the hook

F. Once unhooked, gently place the fish back into the water. If the fish does not swim away move it slowly back and forward to force water through its gills

G. Consider pinching off or flattening hook barbs when the bite is hot and fish will be released

H. If deeply hooked, cut your line as close as possible and release the fish. Your hook will rust out in a short time

I. Use black thin wire hooks. Do not use nickel (silver) hooks, as they take much longer to rust out. Never tie your flies on stainless hooks as they will stay in the fish for a very long time.

J. Keep fish that are deeply hooked and bleeding profusely for the dinner table

K. Five-inch or longer stainless forceps work best for removing hooks

L. Only keep what you are certain to eat fresh and a small amount to freeze.

By releasing our fish back into the ocean we will help to upgrade our current fish stock and provide better fishing for everyone in the future. Please practice: catch and release!

Fishing Etiquette and Safety

Surf fishing is a great way to burn off the pent up frustration that arises from our daily lives. Sometimes we even keep a fish to enjoy for supper. Although the beach can sometimes include confrontation we are reminded that it is there for recreation and if we follow a few simple rules we will always leave the beach with a feeling of peace and well being.

Here are a few rules I fish by:
When you go to the beach remember you're there for recreation and not confrontation. Every so often we run into some bonehead and have to remind ourselves to keep cool. Be patient and enjoy yourself.

From Seattle to San Felipe Mexico there are more than 3,000 miles of surf fishing coastline. Feel free to spread out and try new areas. If you see someone fishing the beach give him or her space to enjoy themselves. If you choose to fish near them, let's say from the rocks or on the beach, take a moment to ask them for their permission. If they say no, move on. Most often they'll say yes and may let you in on what they're doing to be successful.

When dealing with swimmers and surfers here are a few things to remember:

Be respectful: Most swimmers and surfers have little knowledge of fishing and don't know when they're in danger or in your way. If you can move a bit, or wait for the drift to take them away, you'll be able to get back to fishing in no time.

Give way to the crowd: If you approach the beach and find it crowded with swimmers and surfers, don't fish there. Find another place to fish or return later once they're gone.

Let them know you're there: If swimmers or surfers paddle out right where you are fishing let them know with a call or whistle and point out as to where your line is. Most of the time they will move on down the beach. If they don't, you move on.

Remove *all* of your trash when you leave the beach. This is my biggest regret of being a fisherman—seeing all the trash anglers' leave behind. So take all of your trash with you and dispose of all leftover bait, as it will attract birds and rats if left on the rocks or beach. At the end of a session I will often have a bag along to pick up trash left by others as I make my way back to my vehicle. I'm not here to clean up the entire beach, but every little bit we do helps ourselves and others enjoy our trips to the shore.

It's good to remember that we are all here to enjoy the ocean and we all have a right to it. With courtesy and a smile it will be much easier for us to enjoy the beach and have some fun too!

Chapter 9

SURF FISH ROAD TRIPS

In This Chapter
Jalama Beach
Refugio State Beach
Emma Wood State Beach
Bolsa Chica State Beach
Carlsbad State Beach

All the way from the cold of Canada to the warm tip of Baja, the West Coast has more than 3,000 miles of shoreline for surf fishing. Although there are hundreds of great places to fish these are a few of my favorites in Southern California:

Jalama Beach

Jalama is one of the most popular camping and fishing beaches on the West Coast. Just one hour north of Santa Barbara, this beach is tucked in between Vandenburg Airforce Base and the Cojo Ranch. The closest town is Lompoc home to the Air Force and civilians that work on ranches and the military base.

I've been camping here since 1975 and it has changed very little. Reservations are still not accepted (except for 2 group areas) so remember it's first-come first-served. The closest alternate camping area is more than 20 mile away so be sure to call the ranger hotline the day before to check for the possibility of vacancies. If the beach is full or you prefer to stay in a hotel the small town of Lompoc, just five miles from the turnoff (20 miles from the park), has everything you'll need.

We first came here to surf but quickly learned how good the perch fishing could be. The beach offers both sand and rock areas that hold fish. There are more than 4 miles of beach stacked to the gills with barred surfperch, bass and halibut. Monster perch roam just in front of the campground—so come prepared for a fight!

Fish you'll find here: Barred surfperch, buttermouth perch, calico bass, rock bass, cabezon, halibut and smelt.

Tackle you'll need here: Light to heavy tackle works here. When fishing the beach I suggest 6lb mono on a light action 8' rod. If you're fishing near or on the rocks move up to 12-15lb mono—and keep a lot of terminal tackle handy!

Areas you'll want to fish: Fishing along the entire 4 miles of beach is spectacular—but here are a few of my favorite spots: Just 1 mile south of the campground you'll find Tarantula Point. The point is a large mass of rocks that juts out into the pacific. You may fish on both sides of it for perch, bass and halibut but be aware of the many snags. I have had my best luck here during calm swells in the summer. Still farther South is Point Conception. It's a long 10-mile walk but along the way you will find many secluded beaches offering both open sand and rocky areas to fish.

North of the campground the beach stretches out for about a mile before you reach a large fence that secures the airbase. Near where the fence begins you will find good fishing right where rocks begin and sand ends.

Last, and probably most significant, is the beach right in front of the campground. Fish both straight out and just to the North where the creek meets the ocean. Some of our best fishing has been right in this area—and close to home!

Getting There

From Santa Barbara travel north on Highway 101 until you pass Gaviota Beach. After turning inland exit traveling West on Highway 1. Jalama Road is 16 miles West and is marked by a small sign. Turn southwest on Jalama Road and drive 14 miles to the park. If you enter Lompoc you've gone too far. Backtrack 5 miles and you'll find the entrance.

Facilities: Fully stocked store and restaurant, fire pits, hot freshwater pay showers, bathrooms, picnic tables, BBQ facilities, public phone (as cell phones don't work here) self-contained and tent camping.

How to Reserve Your Spot

Reservations are *NOT ACCEPTED* except for group areas.
Jalama Beach County Park
Recorded information: 805-736-6316
Group Reservations: 805-934-6211
www.sbparks.org

Refugio State Beach

Refugio State Beach, just north of Santa Barbara, is both a great camping and fishing destination. As with most of our State parks, camping fills up quickly and a reservation is always recommended.

Refugio's camping area is spread out across a flat wash area and fronts the ocean. Facilities here are great for both tent and motorhome campers. A small store, flush toilet restrooms and showers are available. All campsites include a fire pit and picnic table. Most campsites are no more than 3 minutes from the sand. There is quite a bit of shade for camping here and open access to the beach.

Fishing here is great for a variety of surf fish. The beach is made up of both rocks and sandy areas. Fishermen hike in both directions from the park to look for fish along miles of beach.

Fish you'll find here: Barred surfperch, buttermouth perch, halibut, cabezon, calico and bull bass

Tackle you'll need here: I would upsize tackle here using 6lb mono on an 8' light action rod for both bait and grubs. When the water is clean here of debris this is also a good area for a surf caster. Use a 10' rod loaded with 20lb mono on a spinning or conventional reel. Using the dropper loop setup and a 4-ounce sinker cast this rig out and put it in the rod holder while fishing the beach with a smaller rod. Look back to check the rod, every once in a while, and don't be surprised when a nice halibut, bass or shark jump on your line.

For fishing halibut in this area (consider using hard baits such as Lucky Craft® or Rapala® lures) I would suggest using a heavier setup with 8-12lb mono matched with an 8-9' medium action (6-18lb rated steelhead rod). Both spinning and casting reels work well with this setup.

Areas you'll want to fish: Great fishing spots are both north and south of the campground. Take time during low tide to walk the beach. Look for the numerous finger reefs that point straight offshore. Line these reefs up with a landmark on the cliffs and return at high tide to fish between the reefs.

When you encounter kelp walk until you find where it ends. There will usually be a break between clumps of debris. Fish in between these masses of kelp and along their edges. This is where you'll find the fish!

Getting There

From Santa Barbara, drive North on U.S. 101 for 23 miles to the Refugio State Beach exit. Exit here and take the road to the west (left) and drive a short distance to the beachside campground.

Facilities: 67 camping sites for self-contained vehicles and tents, fire pits, freshwater (pay) showers, restrooms, picnic tables, BBQ facilities, and summer convenience store.

How To Reserve Your Spot

www.reserveamerica.com
Overnight Camping Fees: $20- $30/ night
Daily Parking (2010) $15.00
Park information: 805-968-1033 / 805-585-1850

Emma Wood State Beach

Emma Wood State Beach is just two miles north of downtown Ventura. Surfers know this spot as "Ventura Overhead", popular for its outside and inside reef breaks.

What makes Emma Wood good for surfing also makes it exceptional for fishing. The two huge offshore reefs are a perfect breeding ground for surf fish. Both are accessible for fishing with the inside reef being best at high tide and the outer reef accessible only at low tides. The beach here consists of both rocks and sand areas with a great number of tide pools filled with marine creatures.

Camping here is limited. The good news is you're very close to the surf. The bad, only self-contained vehicles can camp here and there's little relief from the road noise.

Overshadowing its camping drawbacks, Emma Wood State Beach offers the widest variety of surf fish on the coast. Perch and croaker are common here but don't be surprised when you hook into a halibut or white seabass that come inside the reefs to spawn.

Fish you'll find here: Barred surfperch, croaker, cabezon, rock bass, sculpin, white seabass, halibut, leopard shark, soupfin shark, and the occasional corbina.

Tackle you'll need here: Emma wood offers both light and heavy tackle applications. This is a perfect spot to throw out the heavy rod and put it in the sand spike while you take the light rod and fish up and down the beach.

Fish a light rod (4-8lb test) inside from the beach. Cast a heavy (20-40lb) conventional outfit at low tide to the outer reef. At night, fish the heavy out fit with no weight, an 8/0 hook and half a mackerel or bonito and let the waves take your bait in and out as you wait for a monstrous shark to jump on.

Areas you'll want to fish: From the Ventura river mouth to well above the campground you will find great fishing opportunities. There are both rock and kelp areas separated by sand. Fish the edges where sand meets rock and try to draw the fish out of the structure and onto your bait.

There are both an inner and an outer reef at the point. The inner reef fishes well at high tide while the outer reef is most accessible at low tide. You can fish this area with a heavy action rod and rod holder while also using a light-line combo to target fish near shore.

Getting There

From Ventura drive north on U.S. 101 for three miles where you will find the State Beach exit. After exiting, drive under the freeway and continue for one-half mile to the park entrance.

Facilities: Chemical toilets, 90 camping sites for self-contained vehicles. Many sites are not level and may contain a mixture of asphalt, dirt, cobble and ocean debris. Be forewarned that an extreme high tide or big surf may close the park.

How To Reserve Your Spot
www.reserveamerica.com
(Self-contained vehicles only)
Overnight Camping Fees: $20- $35/ night
Park information: 805-968-1033 or 805-585-1850

Bolsa Chica State Beach

Bolsa Chica State Beach offers some of the best surf fishing on the West Coast. Designed by the Army Corp of Engineers, the huge Bolsa estuary was connected to the ocean by an inlet in 2006. The estuary bays are full of spawning surf fish. Working as a supply route, a veritable "fish superhighway", the inlet acts as the perfect stocking system for the entire Orange County coast.

Bolsa Chica State Beach is located between Warner Ave. and Golden West Street along Pacific Coast Highway in Huntington Beach. With more than five miles of beach and over 200 fire pits it's a great place to spend time with your family and have a chance at some of the best surf fishing on the coast.

The park opens at 6am and closes at 10pm. Its facilities include fresh water showers, bathrooms, fire pits, overnight camping for self contained vehicles, park benches and miles of sandy beach great for fishing, surfing and relaxing. Bolsa Chica State Beach offers visitor's miles of sandy beach, hundreds of fire pits, camping and great surf fishing, beach combing and surfing.

Fish you'll find here:
Walleye surfperch, buttermouth perch, zebra perch, barred surfperch, corbina, croaker, halibut, leopard sharks, rays and various sharks.

Tackle you'll need here:
On the sandy beach I like to use an 8' light-action rod matched with 4-6lb mono on a spinning reel. For fishing from or adjacent to rocks I'll upsize my equipment and go with a bit stiffer rod and 6-8lb mono.

Areas you'll want to fish:
For summertime bait, sand crabs are plentiful all along this three mile State Park. When fishing the open beach you may find surfperch, corbina, croaker and various sharks. If you plan to fish in or near the inlet you'll also have a good chance of catching a halibut.

The open beach seems to fish best at high tide while the inlet seems best at peak high and peak low tides. Take some time to search around at low tide for troughs and holes. Line them up with something on shore and go back at high tide to fish them.

Getting There

Location: Huntington Beach, CA. On Pacific Coast Hwy. Between Golden West to the South and Warner Ave. to the North. Hours: 6am to 10pm Monday thru Sunday. Gates close at 9pm Facilities: Firepits, freshwater showers, bathrooms, picnic tables, BBQ facilities, camping for self-contained vehicles
Phone: 714-846-3460

How To Reserve Your Spot

www.reserveamerica.com
(Self-contained vehicles only)
Overnight Camping Fees: $35- $50/ night
Daily Parking (2010) $15.00

South Carlsbad State Beach

South Carlsbad State Beach is just one of the many great surf fishing spots in San Diego County. This state park offers year round fishing. Located in Northern San Diego Carlsbad features swimming, surfing, skin diving, fishing, camping and picnicking. The large bluff top campground is very popular, especially in summer. Stairs lead to the beach.

Located at 7201 Carlsbad Blvd. in Carlsbad California this State park offers bluff top campsites with beautiful views of the Pacific. The campground is well designed with clean new bathrooms (with flush toilets!), showers, dump station, store and most campsites are just steps from the beach.

Fish you'll find here:
Barred surfperch, walleye surfperch, corbina, halibut, croaker, various sharks

Tackle you'll need here:
This spot is mostly sand beach with a few small rocks. A light action 8' rod matched with 4 or 6lb mono-filled spinning reel.

Areas you'll want to fish:
For bait look on the beach between the access stairs during high tide periods. Many times the crabs will be located near areas of small rocks. For fishing the best idea is to stroll the beach and fan

cast for fish. There is very little structure here so most fish will be in holes or the inshore trough.

Scope out this beach at low tide and line those spots up with something on the cliffs so you can go back at high tide and fish right in the trough.

Getting There
South Carlsbad State Beach
7201 Carlsbad Blvd.
Carlsbad CA 92008

From INTERSTATE 5 take exit - Palomar Airport Rd.
Go west to Carlsbad Blvd. - South
Turn slightly right onto ramp.
Merge onto Carlsbad Blvd –South and continue 1.6 miles to Campground.
(Campground Entrance NOT accessible from Poinsettia Ave.)
Campground Address: 7201 Carlsbad Blvd.
Mailing Address: 2680 Carlsbad Blvd. Carlsbad, CA 92008

How To Reserve Your Spot
www.reserveamerica.com

Facilities: 222 campsites available for self-contained vehicles and tents. Most campsites are improved dirt just off the paved entrance road. There are several handicap sites with easy access to bathrooms and other amenities. It can be warm here in spring, summer and fall so be sure to bring umbrellas for the beach and a pop-up cover for camp. Reservations can be made up to seven months in advance and are advised as the park many times sells out. Most sites are separated by a large hedge and have a modest amount of privacy. All sites have a large picnic table and fire pit with barbecue. Showers and bathrooms are not far away and campers can access the beach via two long rows of cliff side stairs.

Overnight Camping Fees: $35-$50/ night
Daily Parking (2010) $15.00
Park information: 760-438-3143 or 619-688-3260

Appendix I

PREPARING FOR THE BEACH

There's now doubt you'll develop your own style when it comes to surf fishing but here are a few tips I use to help me get ready for the beach:

1. *Start preparing the night before.* Being well organized and properly prepared will ensure that your fishing will provide you with the best opportunity for success. (In regard to checking the gear I will do so days in advance. Check your reels for smooth operation (especially the drag, which is critical in maintaining control of the fish on light-line) Also, make certain your line is in good condition.

2. *Get your bait ready.* If you're using clams or mussel, shuck them and put them in small zip top bags before you go. You don't want to be fiddling with a knife in the dark or when you could be catching fish. If you have live ghost shrimp put them in a small container of cool water. Place a frozen bottle in the water over night and you will have lively, crisp shrimp in the morning. If you have collected sand or sidewinder crabs, flush them with cool salt water twice per day and keep them in a cool place until use. When it comes to grubs and artificial lures know in advance what you want to use. Don't waste time fooling around with your bait at the beach.

3. *Pre-tie leaders.* Tie several lengths of leader with different sizes and types of hooks. Use leader material appropriate for the areas you will fish and the target species. Organizing these on leader holders will keep them from getting tangled and make it easy to replace broken or knotted leaders. Fewer knots to tie on the beach equals more time for fish on the line.

4. *Figure out what to wear in advance.* You may like waders or a wet suit but here's how I usually dress for the beach: In winter, I always try to stay dry. It seems the best time to fish is often at high tide so little wading is needed. I'll wear sweats or jeans, old tennis shoes and socks. There's a good chance your feet will get wet so an old pair of shoes is best. If you prefer you can wear calf length "mucking boots" just watch the surf so it doesn't come over the top of your boot. On top, wear enough layers and you'll be warm at sunrise and can peel down as the beach warms up. In spring, summer and fall I like to wade and fish at all tides. Shorts and trunks work great with bare feet or strap sandals (if you're fishing on the rocks). A "T" shirt accompanied by a light jacket or windbreaker with pockets

to hold your gear. Just remember while wading barefoot in summer to shuffle your feet to warn any stingrays of your approach.

5. *Get your camera and batteries ready.* I like to use a plastic zip bag to carry my camera in. This helps keep the sand and salt off your equipment. Always clean your lens the night before with an appropriate lens cleaning paper or cloth to be sure there are no spots on the lens to obscure your pictures.

6. *Organize and put your tackle in a tackle bag.* I like to use a small bag that straps around my waist or a tackle wallet that hangs from around my neck. Inside the bag I'll have:

> 10 swivels
> 10 beads (5 clear/ 5 red)
> Small spool of 6lb fluorocarbon leader
> 6 Drop shot hooks
> 6 Worm/Ghost shrimp hooks
> 6 Pre-tied leaders on 2 leader holders
> 1 Small zip bag with grubs and flies
> 1 **Small zip bag with hot sauce for dippin'**
> 6 Egg sinkers $1/4^{th} - 3/4^{th}$ oz

7. *Check the beach conditions.* Look at weather, wind and swell reports on sites like: www.fishthesurf.com, www.swellwatch.com , www.surfline.com, www.weather.com (and many others). From these sites you'll learn how to plan for the beach based on the conditions. For example, if it is going to be windy I would look for a spot near a jetty protected from wind, or on a day with strong surf, I might start fishing in a sheltered area or protected cove. It's smart to check out a live camera which

focus on the beach you will be fishing the day (or several days) before you go. This way you can see the size of the surf, know when it gets crowded and the morning and afternoon wind conditions.

8. *Check the swell conditions.* The size of surf is always important to surf fishermen. You want the surf to be between one and five feet. If the surf is too small little water will be moving and you'll find few fish. Waves over five feet will create a current that makes catching fish much more difficult. You will also want to determine the direction of the swell. If the swell is from the south you can assume it will be pushing warmer water up the coast (which is good) but may also make some areas unfishable. Take time to familiarize yourself with your favorite spots during different swell conditions. By checking websites like www.wetsand.com you can use graphic forecast models to predict swell size and direction days before heading down to the beach.

9. *Check the tides.* Only the use of sharp hooks is more important than this one. Knowing the best tide for your spot will be the difference between catching fish and getting "skunked." I use a *tide graph* like the one on my site so I can see the tides over a seven-day period at a glance. This makes it easier to know when the right tides are for the best fishing and will allow you to plan ahead with confidence. I've found that if the beach has never been dredged and has natural structure (like kelp and rocks) it can be fished at both high and low tides. But in areas that have been dredged I mostly fish between two hours before to two hours after the high tide. This is when the greatest amount of structure is covered by water and provides inshore troughs that hold fish. When fishing for corbina a low tide going to a high

10. tide is a good time as the fish regularly come up and over the crab beds to feed. When fishing for perch I like a high going to a low tide so as to drag my bait down the sand into their trough. For halibut, the best tide may be at peak high and peak low tides when the water is most calm. "Them'z lazy critters!"

11. *Check the weather.* Find out if a storm is coming or if the wind is going to be up. There's no reason to go to the beach as waves of rain roll in--but there are times, just hours or days before a storm, when the change in barometric pressure caused by the approaching low triggers a signal for fish to eat and then go wide open!

12. *Also look at sites* like: www.scsurffishing.com www.fishingnetwork.net, www.allcoast.com, www.bloodydecks.com for catch, conditions and pictures of fish caught today. These sites will help you keep up with exactly what is being caught today. You can also see the beach conditions and get some great tips on what's working best in the surf for bait, tackle and rigging.

13. *You're almost there. Now pack the car and get ready for the beach!*

What I Take To The Beach

Fishing rod, reel and fresh line
Tackle bag (with tackle listed above)
License
Bait
Bait bucket
Small cooler
2 frozen water bottles for cooler
Water bottle for refreshment
Measuring tape
Line clippers
Suntan lotion
Sunglasses (polarized)
Hat
Camera with fresh batteries
Small pocket rag for hands
Hemostats or Pliers for hook removal

Appendix II

How to build your own Ghost Shrimp Pump ("Slurp Gun")

By Dana Rea

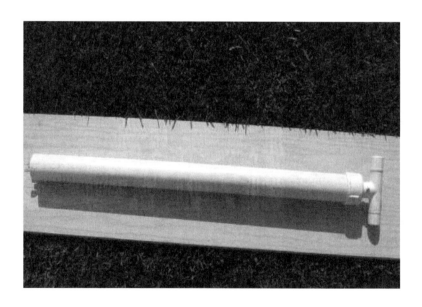

Ghost Shrimp can be found in many places along the Southern California coastline. Adult Ghost Shrimp grow to about 4 ½" long and the males tend to have one claw that is considerably larger than the other.

The color of a Ghost Shrimp will range from being pure white to a deep rich orange or even a combination of both colors.

Ghost Shrimp live in sandy and muddy intertidal zones, bays and estuaries. They dig burrows often shared with other fish and invertebrates. They eat plankton and "detritus", which consists of small pieces of organic plant and animal waste.

The best place to find shrimp is along beaches and bays that have exposed mud flats during low tides. I've found that low tide is a must to finding Ghost Shrimp in quantity. A negative low tide is best, but not absolutely critical.

You'll know a good location by the number of burrows.

Take a look at the photo below to see a good example of what these burrows look like and what you'll be looking for:

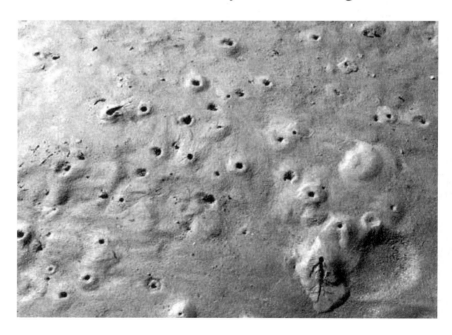

The best burrows for collecting are in "wet zones" of any mud flat. The mud should still be saturated with water, as this will also make your pumping a lot easier.

Ghost Shrimp make fantastic bait for fishing off the beaches of Southern California so why not catch your own!

All sorts of surf fish species including corbina, surfperch, halibut, sargo, spotfin and yellowfin croaker can be caught while using this easily obtained surf fishing "candy" bait!

One of the best ways to do this is with a Ghost Shrimp Pump also known as a "Slurp Gun".

Basically, this gun is nothing more than a suction device that produces a vacuum when the handle is pulled.

When the bottom of the Ghost Shrimp Pump is placed over the hole of the Ghost Shrimp burrow and the handle is pulled up, all the sand is sucked up and hopefully the ghost shrimp is sucked up as well!

When the contents are expelled the angler searches through the discarded mud or sand for ghost shrimp. It's as simple as that!

Place your pump over the center of the burrow and pull the handle. This will cause the pump to dig into the mud while pulling the burrow's contents into the chamber.

In one swift motion pull the pump out, aim it to the side and push the handle down. This will expel the contents.

Repeat a few times in the same hole as needed. Most ghost shrimp burrows have multiple entrances and exits. If you haven't found shrimp in three or four pumps move on.

Be sure to have a container to carry your shrimp in (for example, a waist bait bucket). And don't forget to rinse them off thoroughly before leaving the bay.

Be sure to go back and check the holes you pumped a few minutes before, as sometimes ghost shrimp are easily missed in the mud and occasionally come to the surface if their burrow has collapsed.

Remember that these little guys are a vital part of the ecosystem so don't wipe out every burrow in a small area and never take more than you need for that day.

Try to space out your collecting over a large area.

I recommend that you return any egg-laden females and the largest shrimp you catch back to the hole from which it came. That way we can be sure there will be bait for future trips to the beach!

Kids love collecting ghost shrimp, so don't be afraid to let them try it! Just keep a safe eye on them at all times and remember some shrimp have large claws and can pinch hard enough to break the skin.

I believe current California law specifies that the "capture limit" of Ghost Shrimp is 50, but always be sure to check current DFG regulations for any updated information just to be on the safe side. You must have a valid fishing license in your possession to collect ghost shrimp. You can find the current regulation here: http://www.dfg.ca.gov/regulations/

Shrimp pumps are very easy and inexpensive to make and most anyone who can follow these simple directions should be able to build one in a no time and save oneself some money!

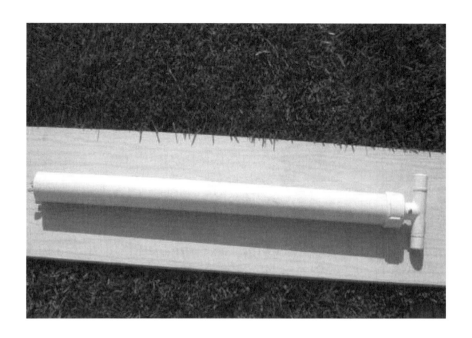

Here's a parts list of what you're going to need to make one like the one depicted:

I purchased all of this at Home Depot for about $17.00

1- 2" x 36" piece of PVC
1- 3/4" x 36" piece of PVC
1 - 3" x 1/2" piece of PVC
2- 1 1/2" pieces of 3/4" PVC
1- 2" PVC cap (non threaded)
3- 3/4" PVC caps (non threaded)
1- 3/4 "PVC tee (non threaded)
1- 2" rubber test plug (for PVC)
1- 1 1/2" metal washer with a 3/8" hole
1- 2" x 5/32" machine screw & nut
1- PVC Primer

1- PVC cement (I used "Weld-On" PVC 2700 Clear)

Note: The test plug should come with plug, bolt, washer and wing nut as shown here:

Make sure that you examine your test plug. It should be the rubber type, not plastic. Some of them come with a washer on top that is larger than 2". Replace it with one that is 1 1/2" in diameter that has a 3/8" hole and is of the same thickness.

Use too small of a washer and the squeezing action of the test plug will not work as well. You can also just grind or cut down the original washer to a 1 1/2" diameter (as I marked) if you prefer.

It is recommended that you "dry fit" your components prior to application of primer and that you allow the primer to "soften" the PVC for about 30 seconds before you apply the cement.

Step #1:
(Handle Assembly)

1. Apply PVC primer/cement to approximately half of one of the 1 1/2" pieces of 3/4" PVC and insert the glued piece half way into one side of the 3/4" tee.

2. Now apply PVC primer/cement to the other half (one end) of the inserted piece and slide one of the 3/4" caps onto that portion.

3. Repeat the same process on the other side of the tee handle.

4. Drill a 3/16" hole in the center of the neck of the 3/4" tee

5. Take the 3" piece of 1/2" PVC and primer/cement it inside the top of the 36" piece of 3/4" PVC. Make sure it is flush with the top of the 3/4" piece when inserted.

(Note: I added the 1/2" insert to give extra support to where I will later attach the handle)

Once the caps have been attached to the 3/4" tee, the handle should appear as it does below:

Note: You can make this pump WITHOUT the caps and WITHOUT the screw and WITHOUT the 1/2" reinforcement... (Just glue the t-handle to the top of the 36" piece of 3/4" PVC)

I added the caps as a way to make the handle a bit wider for a better grip. This will result in less fatigue while pumping.

Rather than just attaching the handle with glue, I choose to use a machine screw to make the handle removable so the gun can be cleaned easily (*Highly recommended*).

I added the 1/2" PVC reinforcement inside the 3/4" piece as a way to make the top of the neck where the handle attaches sturdier.

Step #2:
(Drilling and attaching the 2" cap)

1. Take the 2" cap and find and mark the dead center of the cap.

2. Drill a 1 1/6" inch hole in the dead center of the cap.

The cap should appear like the one shown below when you are done. I used the tool shown here (hole saw), but you can also drill a 3/4" hole and then file it out to 1 1/16", or use a "step-drill".

IMPORTANT: Be careful to make and drill the hole at dead center.

2. Once the hole is drilled properly, apply PVC primer/cement to the inside of the 2" cap and attach it to your 36" piece of 2" PVC.

3. Now slide the 3/4" tee handle onto your 36" piece of 3/4" PVC. Using the hole that you already drilled in the tee handle as a guide, drill a 3/16" hole thru all of the pieces

4. Insert a 2" x 5/32" machine screw & nut and attach the handle.

You should now have two assembled pieces, again similar to the ones shown below:

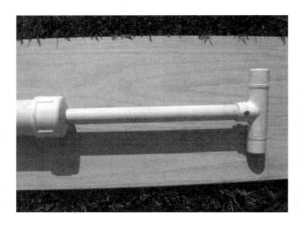

Step #3:

Pump Piston assembly:

1. Take the remaining 3/4" cap and drill a 3/8" hole dead center.

2. The "test plug" comes with a square shouldered (carriage) bolt.

File out the 3/8" hole so the square shouldered bolt fits perfectly once it's installed from the inside of the 3/4" cap (Yes, you'll be making a round hole square)

3. Install the carriage bolt by pushing the bolt thru the cap from the INSIDE of the cap. DO NOT YET ASSEMBLE THE ENTIRE PLUG

4. Next, primer/cement the 36" piece of PVC (with the attached handle) into the inside of the 3/4" cap

5. Now insert the 3/4" piece thru the 2" cap and push all the way down

6. Finally, attach the rest of the "plug" hardware.
(Once assembled, it should appear as shown below)

7. Use the wingnut to adjust the plug so it makes a good seal yet allows the handle and rod to be pumped up and down smoothly. Adjust the plug once you're in the field. Thick sand, mud or lack of water may require you to loosen and retest the plug.

You're done!

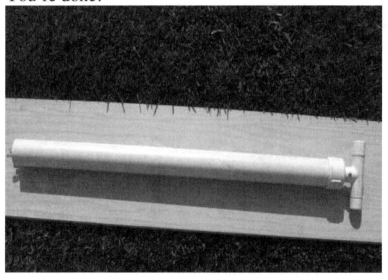

Note: There are certainly better ways and EASIER ways to make a "slurp gun"... this just happens to be how I made mine.

There are all sorts of people on the web selling slurp guns, even selling "plans" on how to build a slurp gun... but if you do a little searching, all the information on how to build one can be found for free on the web... that's how I learned how to build mine.

This article is published in memoriam to its author Dana "Team57" Rea

Dana Rea of Team57 has researched and written a great article about ghost shrimp and how to build a pump. You can find his article at: www.fishingnetwork.net, www.team57fishing.com Tragically, Dana lost his struggle with heart disease in 2010 and will be greatly missed.

Dana's contributions as a moderator and regular contributor to Fish Taco Chronicles, dozens of fishing seminars, events and as a long time moderator on fishingnetwork.net were a testament to his love for fishing and teaching others. Again, thanks to Dana for his support of surf fishing and the fisherman's right to enjoy the beach. He was a great colleague and an even better friend who will be missed but forever remembered.

Appendix III

Full-Service Tackle Shops with Live Surf Bait

Wylie's Bait and Tackle
18757 Pacific Coast Hwy
Malibu, CA 90265
310-456-2321

Bait: Since 1946 this shop has been a historical landmark in the world of surf fishing. Don't be afraid to ask proprietor Ginny Wylie the hot tip—she's surf fishing royalty and has all the inside info you'll need to make your day on the beach. Long time provider of good bait and great advice look for: Lug worms, mussel, shark bait, anchovey and a steller offering of various surf grubs and free advice.

Paul's Bait and Tackle
803 S. Pacific Ave.
San Pedro, CA 90731
(310) 833-3279
paulsbait@yahoo.com

Bait: Ghost Shrimp, Blood/Lug Worms, Night Crawlers, Clams, Mussel, Frozen Bait, Shark Chum

Norm's Big Fish Bait and Tackle
1780 Pacific Coast Hwy
Seal Beach, CA 90740-6209
(562) 431-0723

Bait: Ghost Shrimp, Mussel, Lug Worms, Clams, Anchovy

Hogan's Bait and Tackle
34320 Pacific Coast Hwy.
Dana Point, CA 92629
(949) 493-3528

Bait: Ghost Shrimp, Lug Worms, Nuclear Worms, Mussel, Anchovy, Squid

Pacific Coast Bait and Tackle
2110 S Coast Hwy Ste E
Oceanside, CA 92054
(760) 439-3474
PacificCoastBaitAndTackle@gmail.com

Bait: Bloodworms, Mussel (fresh and frozen), Anchovy, Sardine, Squid, Shrimp, Clams, Mackerel, Lug Worms
Website: http://www.pacificcoast-baitandtackle.com

Appendix IV

2010
CALIFORNIA STATE FISHING RECORDS
SALT WATER

Barracuda, California 15 lb 15 oz San Onofre Aug. 24, 1957 C. O. Taylor
Bass, Giant Sea* 563 lb 8 oz Anacapa Island Aug. 20, 1968 James D. McAdams Jr.
Bass, Barred Sand 13 lb 3 oz Huntington Flats Aug. 29, 1988 Robert Halal
Bass, Kelp 14 lb 7 oz San Clemente Island Jul. 30, 1958 C. O. Taylor
Bass, Spotted Sand 6 lb 12 oz Newport Bay Oct. 1, 1994 Matt Bergherm
Bonito, Pacific 21 lb 5 oz 181 Spot Oct. 19, 2003 Kim Larson
Cabezon 23 lb 4 oz Los Angeles Apr. 20, 1958 Bruce Kuhn
Corbina, California 7 lb 1 oz Newport Harbor May 30, 2005 Scott Matthews
Croaker, Spotfin 14 lb 0 oz Playa del Rey Sep. 24, 1951 Charles Dusart
Croaker, Yellowfin 3 lb 14 oz Santa Monica Beach Oct. 8, 2000 Fred Oakley
Dolphinfish 66 lb 0 oz 209 Spot Sep. 9, 1990 Kim Carson
Flounder, Starry 11 lb 4 oz San Simeon Aug. 29, 1993 Steve Doshier
Greenling, Kelp 2 lb 9 oz San Simeon Jul. 23, 1993 Ray Hardy
Halibut, California 58 lb 9 oz Santa Rosa Island Jun. 26, 1999 Roger W. Borrell
Jacksmelt 1 lb 8 oz San Nicholas Island May 12, 1998 William J. Rogers
Lingcod 56 lb 0 oz Crescent City Jul. 12, 1992 Carey Mitchell
Mackerel, Jack 5 lb 8 oz Huntington Beach Sep. 1, 1988 Joe Bairian
Mackerel, Pacific (Chub) 2 lb 8 oz Mission Beach Nov. 11, 2005 Thomas Hilgert
Marlin, Blue 692 lb 0 oz Balboa Aug. 18, 1931 A. Hamann
Marlin, Striped 339 lb 0 oz Catalina Island Jul. 4, 1985 Gary Jasper
Opah 163 lb 0 oz Port San Luis Oct. 8, 1998 Tom Foran
Opaleye 6 lb 4 oz Los Flores Creek May 13, 1956 Leonard Itkoff
Perch, Pile 1 lb 15 oz Long Beach Feb. 26, 2007 Ronald Schmidt
Perch, Black 1 lb 11 oz San Carlos Beach May 14, 2006 Mathew Michie
Prickleback, Monkeyface 6 lb 1 oz Pescadero Feb. 7, 2005 Kirk Lombard
Ray, Bat 181 lb 0 oz Huntington Beach Jul. 24, 1978 Bradley Dew
Rockfish, Black 9 lb 2 oz S.F. Light Station Sep. 3, 1988 Trent Wilcox
Rockfish, Blue 3 lb 14 oz San Carpoforo Oct. 14, 1993 Terry Lamb Jr.
Rockfish, Bocaccio 17 lb 8 oz Point St Georges Reef Oct. 25, 1987 Sam Strait
Rockfish, Bronzespotted 14 lb 8 oz Cherry Bank Feb. 22, 1997 Conor Gorey
Rockfish, Brown 5 lb 15 oz Farallon Islands Feb. 28, 2002 Mike Librero
Rockfish, Canary 6 lb 15 oz Usal Beach Sep. 30, 2001 Kevin Kerns
Rockfish, China 3 lb 4 oz Russian River Jul. 24, 1998 Joe Newman

Rockfish, Copper 8 lb 5 oz Pigeon Point Aug. 18, 1985 Kenny Aab
Rockfish, Cowcod* 21 lb 14 oz Hidden Reef Aug. 10, 1998 Carlos A. Herrera
Rockfish, Grass 5 lb 6 oz Trinidad Jul. 14, 2006 Kyle Spragens
Rockfish, Greenspotted 2 lb 5 oz Piedras Blancas Jun. 24, 2005 John Wallick
Rockfish, Olive 5 lb14 oz St.Augustine Reef, Santa Barbara Nov. 21, 1991 Haady Forbes
Rockfish, Treefish 4 lb 3 oz Malibu Aug. 9, 2003 Joseph E. Kokrak
Rockfish, Vermilion 14 lb 9 oz Morro Bay Jul. 31, 1996 Bobby Cruce
Rockfish, Yelloweye* 18 lb 3 oz Piedras Blancas Apr. 15, 1994 John Cossey
Rockfish, Yellowtail 5 lb 8 oz Alder Ck., Monterey Co. Aug. 4, 1991 Alberto Cortez
Salmon, Chinook (King) 65 lb 4 oz Crescent City Aug. 21, 2002 Franklin T. Cox
Scorpionfish, Calif. (Sculpin) 3 lb 0 oz Silver Strand Beach Dec. 26, 1997 Nathan Weatherson
Seaperch, Barred 4 lb 2 oz Morro Bay Nov. 8 1995 Artie J. Ferguson
Seaperch, Barred 4 lb 2 oz Oxnard Mar. 30, 1996 Fred Oakley
Seaperch, Rubberlip 4 lb 4 oz Monterey Dunes Jun. 24, 1995 Joe Manalac
Seaperch, Striped 2 lb 3 oz Wilson Beach March 24, 2008 Floyd Underwood
Seabass, White 78 lb 0 oz Monterey Bay Apr. 4, 2002 David L. Sternberg
Shark, Blue 164 lb 0 oz Newport Beach Sep. 17, 2006 Shane L. Smith
Shark, Leopard 47 lb 1 oz Palos Verdes Jul. 18, 2007 Ronald Schmidt
Shark, Sevengill 276 lb 0 oz Humboldt Bay Oct. 17, 1996 Cliff Brewer
Shark, Shortfin Mako 1059 lb 6 oz Oxnard Jul. 15, 2006 Marylin Stephens
Shark, Thresher 527 lb 0 oz San Diego Oct. 4, 1980 Kenneth Schilling
Sheephead, California 28 lb 14 oz Paradise Cove Dec. 6, 1978 Tibor Molnar Jr.
Sole, Fantail 8 lb 8 oz San Clemente Island Jun. 6, 2001 Allan Sheridan
Surfperch, Redtail 2 lb 15 oz Klamath Beach June 29, 2003 Edward Mitsui
Swordfish, Broadbill 452 lb 8 oz Catalina Island Sep. 30, 2003 David M. Denholm
Tuna, Albacore 90 lb 0 oz Santa Cruz Oct. 21, 1997 Don Giberson
Tuna, Bigeye 240 lb 0 oz Butterfly Bank Aug. 1, 1987 Steve Hutchinson
Tuna, Bluefin 243 lb 11 oz 277 Spot Sept. 8, 1990 Karl E. Schmidbauer
Tuna, Skipjack 26 lb 0 oz San Diego Aug. 28, 1970 William Hall
Tuna, Yellowfin 239 lb 0 oz Catalina Island Nov. 4, 1984 Ronald R. Howarth
Whitefish, Ocean 13 lb 12 oz Cortes Bank Apr. 23, 1988 Bob Schwenk
Yellowtail 63 lb 1 oz Santa Barbara Is. Jun. 18, 2000 Kwang Nam Lee

*State law presently prohibits the take of giant (black) sea bass, canary cowcod, and yelloweye rockfish. Always check the DFG website for up-to-date laws and closures. This information was found at: http://www.dfg.ca.gov/marine/pdfs/anglingrecords.pdf where you can find the most recent additions to the California sport fishing records.

SURF FISH CALENDAR

FISH	JANUARY	FEBRUARY	MARCH	APRIL	MAY	JUNE	JULY	AUGUST	SEPTEMBER	OCTOBER	NOVEMBER	DECEMBER
CORBINA	☺	☺	☺	☺	☺☺	☺☺☺	☺☺	☺☺	☺☺	☺☺	☺	☺
YELLOWFIN CROAKER	☺	☺	☺	☺	☺☺	☺☺☺	☺☺	☺☺	☺☺	☺☺	☺☺	☺
BARRED SURF PERCH	☺☺☺	☺☺☺	☺☺☺	☺☺	☺☺	☺	☺	☺	☺	☺☺	☺☺☺	☺☺☺
WALLEYE SURF PERCH	☺☺☺	☺☺☺	☺☺☺	☺☺	☺☺	☺	☺	☺	☺	☺☺	☺☺☺	☺☺☺
HALIBUT	☺	☺	☺☺	☺☺	☺☺☺	☺☺	☺☺	☺☺	☺☺	☺☺	☺	☺
SPOTFIN CROAKER	☺	☺	☺	☺☺	☺☺☺	☺☺☺	☺☺	☺☺	☺☺	☺☺	☺	☺

☺   Nothing to write home about but any thing is possible
☺☺   Good solid fishing
☺☺☺   Call the boss and tell him you'll be late for work--it's fishin' time!

SURF BAIT CALENDAR

(Southern California Area: Shows best months for using these natural baits)

BAIT	JANUARY	FEBRUARY	MARCH	APRIL	MAY	JUNE	JULY	AUGUST	SEPTEMBER	OCTOBER	NOVEMBER	DECEMBER
SIDEWINDER CRABS	☺☺☺	☺☺☺	☺☺☺	☺☺	☺	☺	☺	☺	☺	☺	☺☺	☺☺☺
SAND CRABS			☺	☺	☺☺	☺☺☺	☺☺☺	☺☺☺	☺☺	☺		
MUSSEL	☺	☺	☺	☺	☺☺	☺☺☺	☺☺☺	☺☺☺	☺☺☺	☺☺☺	☺☺	☺
GHOST SHRIMP	☺☺	☺☺	☺☺	☺☺	☺☺	☺☺	☺☺	☺☺☺	☺☺☺	☺☺☺	☺☺	☺☺
CLAMS	☺☺☺	☺☺☺	☺☺☺	☺☺	☺☺	☺☺	☺☺	☺☺	☺☺☺	☺☺☺	☺☺☺	☺☺☺
WORMS	☺☺☺	☺☺☺	☺☺☺	☺☺	☺☺	☺☺	☺☺	☺☺	☺☺	☺☺	☺☺☺	☺☺☺
GRUBS	☺☺☺	☺☺☺	☺☺	☺☺	☺☺	☺	☺	☺	☺☺	☺	☺☺	☺☺

☺   Give it a shot I dare you!
☺☺   Good Backup Bait
☺☺☺   *The One and Only*—Start here first!

REFERENCES

To become an even better fisherman check out these great references

Books

Probably More Than You Want To Know About The Fishes Of The Pacific Coast, Milton Love, 1996, ISBN 0-9628725-5-5. A great book with pictures, descriptions and analysis of many West Coast shallow and deep-water fish.

"Behavior and physical factors causing migration and aggregation of the sand crab", Stimpson, on the Internet here: http://www.dfg.ca.gov/marine/status/sand_crab.pdf

The Lore Of Sportfishing, Tre Tryckare, E. Cagner, Frank T. Moss, 1976, Crown Publishing ISBN: 0-517-52109-1. The granddaddy of sportfishing books. Covers almost everything with over 2500 pictures and illustrations.

California Finfish and Shellfish Identification Book, various contributors, California Department of Fish and Game, 2006, ISBN: 0-9722291-1-6. Excellent overview of West Coast fish. Includes information on characteristics, feeding habits, life history and other facts.

Surf Fishing Websites, Blogs, Message Boards

Fish Identification:
http://www.mexfish.com/fish/fish.htm

Surf Fishing Related Websites:
http://www.fishthesurf.com
http://www.pierfishing.com

California Dept. of Fish and Game:
http://www.dfg.ca.gov
Oregon:
http://www.dfw.state.or.us
Washington:
http://wdfw.wa.gov/fishing
Mexico:
http://www.conapescasandiego.org/contenido.cfm?cont=REGULATIONS

Message boards: (pictures, reports, discussion, tips)
http://www.scsurffishing.com
http://www.allcoast.com
http://www.fishingnetwork.net
http://www.bloodydecks.com

Blogs:
http://surffishingreport.blogspot.com

Video: (instruction, entertainment)
http://www.youtube.com

NOTES